Science Investigations

Editors
Walter Kelly, M.A.
Mara Ellen Guckian

Editorial Project Manager
Karen Goldfluss, M.S. Ed.

Editor in Chief
Sharon Coan, M.S. Ed.

Illustrator
Howard Chaney

Cover Artist
Larry Bauer

Art Coordinator
Cheri Macoubrie Wilson

Creative Director
Elayne Roberts

Imaging
Ralph Olmedo, Jr.

Product Manager
Phil Garcia

Publishers
Rachelle Cracchiolo, M.S. Ed.
Mary Dupuy Smith, M.S. Ed.

Author

Robert W. Smith

Teacher Created Materials, Inc.
6421 Industry Way
Westminster, CA 92683
www.teachercreated.com
ISBN-1-57690-506-3
©*1999 Teacher Created Materials, Inc.*
Made in U.S.A.

Table of Contents

Introduction

This introduction offers information about format, layout, materials, grouping suggestions, instructional strategies, and the general nature of constructivist, open-ended, inquiry-based science. The activities are intended to be multi-directional and open-ended in their style. They are true exercises in learning science by doing science.

Format

Each activity in this book is four pages long and moves from simple, introductory projects to more complex ones. Every project has elements which encourage students to build upon previous learning and to develop creative and imaginative variations. Each unit has a concluding activity, open-ended in concept and designed to encourage creative energies and problem-solving skills. This concluding activity can also be used as an authentic assessment vehicle to determine how well students have learned basic concepts and how well they can apply them.

Using the Book

These units can be used in whole-class instructional situations by two-person collaborative teams, by individuals or teams in centers, as project assignments, as GATE activities, and in small group settings. Virtually all the activities require extended time and multiple periods to be done thoroughly.

Constructivist Science

The focus of this book is to provide long-term, inquiry-based science activities. The projects all involve a hands-on, problem-solving approach. Students start with relatively simple, introductory projects and progress to more involved activities which influence them to develop modifications, improvements, variations, and challenging levels of scientific sophistication.

Materials

Each activity indicates materials needed and optional materials that might be substituted. The materials are, in most cases, both easy to acquire and inexpensive. Many of the projects use inexpensive substitutes which make it possible for all students to do the activities on a very modest science budget. For example, wood doweling for building kites can be quite expensive and require other tools. However, the thin stirrers/straws used to make these kites cost only about $3 for over 2,000 straws at discount and membership stores.

Most of the materials detailed in the projects are available as general school supplies. Other supplies include common household items such as plastic garbage bags, food coloring, salt, ammonia, laundry bluing, vinegar, baking soda, vegetable oil, clear plastic water bottles, and similar items.

Introduction *(cont.)*

Materials *(cont.)*

Several items should be available in any school science kit. These include magnifying glasses, eyedroppers, one-ounce (30 mL) graduated plastic measuring cups, flashlight batteries, bulbs, sockets, thin insulated wire, and some animal habitat containers. Science supplies can also be purchased from science supply catalogs distributed by Delta Education, Carolina Biological Supply, and others.

A few disposable supplies used routinely include Styrofoam hamburger trays, plastic and paper cups, several sizes of straws, coffee filters, manila folders or tagboard, and paper towels. These supplies can be purchased in volume inexpensively in discount markets and membership stores.

The fishline can be bought at sports and fishing sections of department stores for less than $2. You may want a few rolls for convenience. Purchase heavier weight line such as 15-to 25-pound test, if available. A few items are best purchased in builder's or home supply stores. The pipe insulation is about $1 a tube. Sand and gravel can also be purchased there.

Grouping Strategies

Most of these activities are ideally done by teams of two students working collaboratively. Putting more students at this age in a group usually leads to more socializing and less work, but the activities can be done by larger groups. The activities can also be done independently by individuals in classroom centers or as individual science projects done at home. You will want to see the final project and a science lab sheet for these if done at home.

These activities are ideal for GATE students and students in need of challenging intellectual fare, but they also stimulate the creative imaginations of students whose talents aren't as obvious. It is often an ideal situation to team a GATE student with a student whose skills are more artistic or manual. You get the leadership, reading skills, and background knowledge of the gifted student combined with the manual dexterity, perseverance, and discipline of the student with an interest in making things with his or her hands.

Dispensing Information

The teacher is not supposed to explain everything that happens in an open-ended, diversity-rich class experience. Encourage students to find the common things which occur in all or most investigations. Condition the students in your classroom to value unique and unusual approaches to investigations. Provide the time and a forum for students to share opinions and the results of their individual or collective investigations.

Introduction *(cont.)*

Extensions

Many students will be inspired to search out more information and activities related to some of the projects and activities in this book. This is an ideal way to encourage students to access other research sources and to simply investigate on their own by making more kite variations, different types of paper planes, more involved circuits, or more unusual applications for the surface tension of water, for example.

Answers Will Vary

Students doing the same project will get a variety of results based on what changes each team or student made in the way they approached the problem. Skill in direction following, creative modifications, and individual differences in manual dexterity will often yield an interesting diversity of final results. This is quite acceptable and to be encouraged. In most of these activities, there is no one right answer and seldom one best way to do something. Creative students will instinctively make changes that improve or sometimes totally redirect the focus of the lesson. Bridges may end up with features that work but aren't specifically mentioned. Towers may have a unique combination of geometric figures. Circuit arrangements may suddenly have half the classroom teams connected to each other and developing their own codes. Students work at different speeds and surprisingly in depth with many of these projects.

Timing

Students often develop a pace entirely their own. Some students will spend an inordinate amount of time on one section and deal only superficially with another. Expect most of these projects to occupy approximately a week with 45-minute daily periods. Some teachers may choose to do them in two or three longer periods. This has advantages for efficient cleanup and storage.

Enjoy

Enjoy the time and the learning experiences that are occurring. Give some direction and help where you have to, but generally circulate among the teams to offer ideas, suggestions, and encouragement. Keep students focused on the main concept and demonstrate how to do things which individual children may find new or unfamiliar. Help the class draw closure on the final discoveries. Provide opportunities for writing and research after each unit. Suggest extensions that students can do. Remind students that science is doing, that scientists fail far more often than they succeed, and that persistence is more valuable than inspiration. (Edison said that "Genius is 99% perspiration and 1% inspiration.") Finally, help students recognize the joy that accompanies successful and challenging learning experiences. Their motto should be "Go for it!"

Roller Derby

Concepts: *motion, momentum, and friction*

Materials: straws (two diameter sizes), small box or hamburger tray, four to eight fast food coffee or soda lids, two large lids, tape, pins, small paper clips, cups, two AA batteries or small penny rolls, balloons, tagboard (6" by 3'), craft stick, scissors

Optional: margarine tubs and lids, wood skewers or pencils, clothespins, large paper clips, straight pins

Roller Car

Study the roller derby models shown here. Choose one model to make. Use coffee or soda lids for the wheels and a straw for the axle. A small box or Styrofoam tray will work for the body of the car.

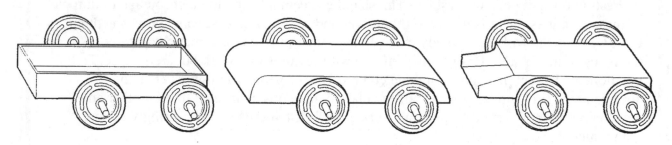

Speedy Axles

You can make a better axle by placing a long, thin straw inside a short, wide straw. Tape the short, wide straw to the bottom of the box. Thread the thin straw through the wide one. Stick each end of the thin straw through a coffee or soda lid. Make sure the thin straw turns easily inside the larger straw.

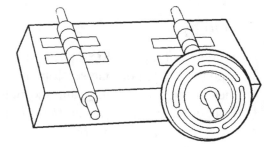

Wild Wheels

You can make the wheels faster and stronger in several ways.

1. Insert one lid inside another and tape them together.
2. Cut a piece of tagboard the same size as each wheel and tape the circular piece inside of each lid.
3. Face two lids next to each other and tape them together.
4. Split the ends of the straw axle that extend beyond the lids and tape these ends securely to the outside of the wheel or use straight pins in the straw axle on each side of the wheel to keep the wheel from bending.
5. Improve the speed and durability of your vehicle by replacing the straw axles with wooden skewers or round pencils. You could also slip these or similar materials into the straws to reinforce the straw axle.

Roller Derby *(cont.)*

Road Test

Use a flat piece of wood about six feet long and three feet wide (2 meters by 1 meter). Elevate one end of the board about three to four feet off the ground. Adjust it firmly so that the board will not slip. A table with legs which can be folded down also works very well. Tape a divider down the middle of the board or table so that you can test two cars at the same time or race against a classmate.

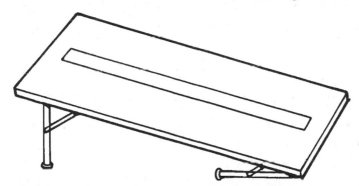

Test your model on the runway. Determine what improvements you can make on the model. Try the modifications shown on this page.

Big Wheels

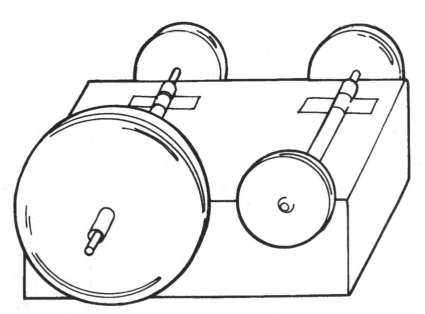

Replace the rear wheels on your derby car with larger lids. Reinforce them the way you did the smaller wheels and attach them to the axle. Test this model on the runway. Determine if the larger wheels increase the car's speed. You can compare the speeds by timing the run, noticing if one car went farther than the other, or by racing your car with and without the big wheels against another car.

Try another set of big wheels on the front of the car. Determine if the speed is improved.

Roller Derby *(cont.)*

The Big Mo

Momentum describes the driving force of a moving object. You may increase the speed of your car by positioning a weight on certain areas of the car. Tape an AA battery or a roll of twenty pennies somewhere on the rear of the car. Test the car on the runway. Compare the speed using another car, timing it, or counting until the car stops.

Try placing the battery in different areas of the car such as the rear, the front, the center, under the car, or elevated above the body of the car. Compare your results. Try a second battery or penny roll. Compare your results.

Three-Wheelers

You can convert your vehicle to a three-wheeler tractor model with any of these modifications:

1. Tape craft sticks to the front of the box. Tape two small paper clips to each side of the craft stick to hold a small straw axle and lid.
2. Cut away a section of the front of the box and attach the smaller axle to the underside of the box. The wheel should fit into the cutaway portion of the box.
3. Elevate the box and tape two larger paper clips to the side of the box so that the loops extend down. Slip each end of the axle into one loop of a paper clip. The body of the vehicle will be above the box.

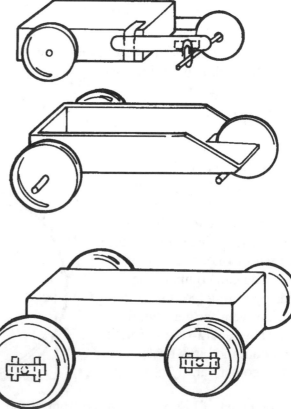

Tractor Treads

Replace your wheel and axle arrangement with cups or margarine tubs. Thread the axles through the center of the bottom of the container and the lid. You may want to tape each straw axle to the lid. You may improve traction by wrapping masking or cloth tape around the container wheels.

Roller Derby *(cont.)*

One on One

Choose the best version of your car for a contest against your classmates. Hold your car with the back wheels against the very top of the ramp in your lane. On command, let your car go. Do not push it.

1. For the first race, the winner is the car with the back wheels that touch the floor first.
2. For the second race, the winner is the car which travels the farthest on the floor before stopping.

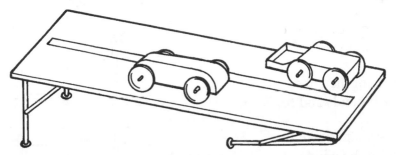

Race your cars again, using a ramp at an incline which is not as steep. Compare your results with the first race.

Automobile Engineer

Build any of the vehicles illustrated here and modify them as you wish or create your own vehicle. Use your experiences to make your vehicle as sturdy and fast as possible.

Test your vehicle on the ramp and race against your classmates.

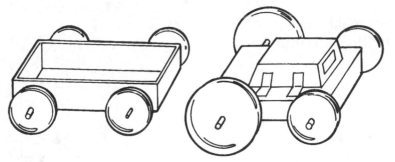

Air-Powered Vehicles

Make a balloon-powered car. Blow up a balloon. Lay the balloon in the body of the car, slip a piece of tubing in the mouth of the balloon, and tape it to the car body. The balloon mouth should be taped snugly over the tubing and face the rear. Keep the balloon closed with a clothespin until ready.

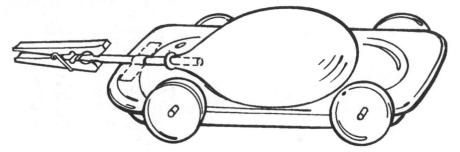

Tallest Towers

Concept: *strength of geometric shapes*

Materials: straws, straight pins, plain paper, scissors, pennies, tape, Styrofoam tray, large paper clips

Cubic Construction

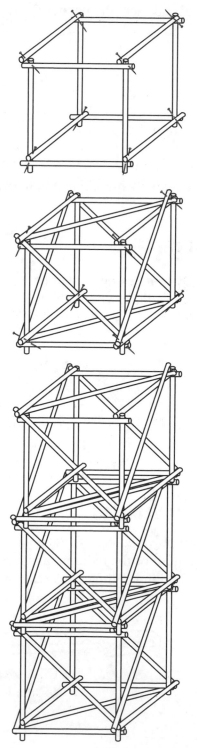

1. Use 12 straws and straight pins to build the cube shown here.

2. Push on the corners of the cube. Notice how easily it bends and folds.

3. Use eight more straws to make this figure stronger. Use the eight extra straws and pins to make the reinforced cube illustrated here.

4. Slit the ends of the straws so that one straw extends into another, making a stronger straw and a piece that fits along the diagonal of the cube. Do this with all four diagonal pieces.

5. Push on the corners of this cube. Notice how much firmer it is than the first one.

Stacking Cubes

1. Use straws and straight pins to make the three-level structure illustrated here.

2. Add three more levels to the structure of the model shown here to create a six-level tower.

Tallest Towers *(cont.)*

Strongest Towers

1. Use a Styrofoam tray or small plate like the one illustrated here to place on top of the tower.

2. Tape or roll 50 pennies or large paper clips in at least 10 packs.

3. Carefully place each roll in the basket on top of your structure until it collapses or the packs roll off. Use more than 10 packs if the structure will support them.

4. Record how many pennies or large paper clips your structure held and compare the results with your classmates.

5. Graph the results for your class.

Stronger Structures

1. Build the six-story structure illustrated here.

2. Remember the tower must stand freely without leaning on anything.

3. Attach the weight tray to the top of your six-story structure. Place the penny or paper clip packs into the basket one at a time until the structure collapses or the weights fall out.

4. Compare results with your three-story structure. Compare results with your classmates.

5. Add as many more stories as you can to this tower. Try to build a 12-story structure.

6. Test the taller structure with the weights. Compare your results with the smaller structures and with your classmates' structures.

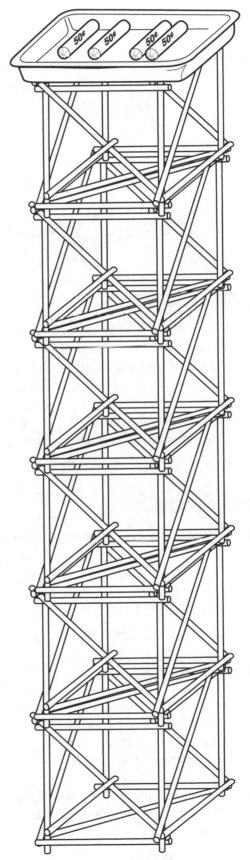

Tallest Towers *(cont.)*

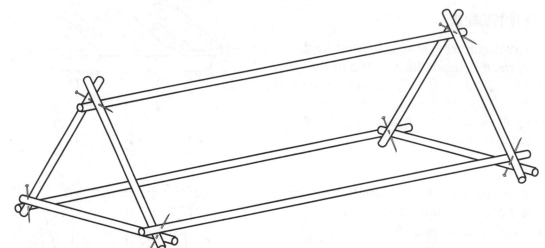

Triangular Towers

The triangular prism is a very strong geometric figure which combines rectangular and triangular shapes. Use straws and pins to make each of the triangular prisms illustrated here.

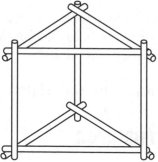

Use the triangular prism design of your choice to make a three-story tower similar to the one pictured here.

Tower of Strength

Attach the tray you used in the previous towers or design a new one to hold the 10 packs of pennies or paper clips. Record how many packs your tower will hold and compare results with your classmates and with your earlier tower designs.

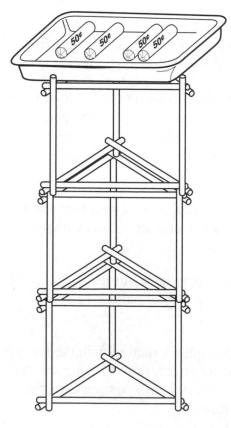

Towering Triangles

Add as many stories to your triangular tower as you can. You may want to use only one style of triangular prism, or you may want to combine two or three styles.

Sketch your tower design on the back of this paper. Test your structure to see how many weights it can hold.

Tallest Towers *(cont.)*

Tallest Free-Standing Tower

All architects and engineers have a limited budget and limited materials.

1. Using only 100 straws and 100 straight pins, build the tallest free-standing tower that you can.
2. Remember, the tower cannot lean against any object, and it will be measured from the base to the top.
3. Using no more than 200 straws and 200 straight pins, make the tallest free-standing tower that you can. Compare your model with those of other classmates. Measure from the base to the highest point of the tower.

Famous Towers

Try to copy any of the towers shown below, modify them, or create a tower entirely from your own imagination.

Sears Tower   Eiffel Tower   Empire State Building   World Trade Center

Boats and Barges

Concepts: *buoyancy and water displacement*

Materials: aluminum foil, modeling clay, toothpicks, straws, tape, crayons, widemouthed cup, plastic bowl, toddler's pool or large tray, small and large paper clips, pennies

Optional: glue, pins, rubber bands, craft sticks, toothpicks, straws, clay, Styrofoam trays and cups, plastic bottles, plastic and paper milk cartons, crayons, tape, aluminum foil, cardboard, pipe cleaners, wire

Aluminum Foil Barges

Barges are flat boats used to carry heavy loads. Choose one of the barges pictured here to build. Use the picture as a model to get started. Make the boat out of aluminum foil about two inches long and one inch wide (5 cm x 2.5 cm).

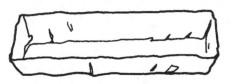

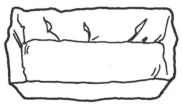

The Proof Is in the Water

Fill a container until the water is three inches (8 cm) deep. Place your boat in the container. Determine how much weight your boat can carry before sinking. Use pennies or large paper clips as weights. Add each weight slowly and carefully. Do several trials and record your results.

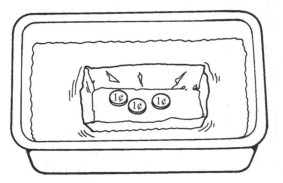

Clay Barges

Make the same style of boat you made before, using one ounce (28 g.) of clay. This is a piece about the size of your little finger. Test your clay barge in the water with the same weights you used with the aluminum barges. Compare your results. Determine which material carried a heavier load.

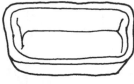

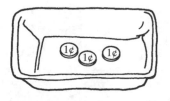

Modifying the Design

Change the design of your clay barge. Test it in the water with the weights. Try several different designs. Include the barge pictured above and your own creations. Record which design carried the most weights.

Boats and Barges *(cont.)*

Crayon Crafts

Add two or three crayons to one of your clay barges like the designs illustrated here. See how many weights this design can carry before it sinks.

Toothpick Tugboats

Make a boat out of toothpicks, using one of the designs shown here. Use glue, clay, or small paper clips to hold the toothpicks together. Test your tugboat to see how many weights it can hold before it sinks.

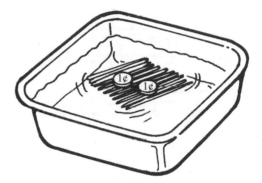

Straw Keelboats

Keelboats were used by pioneers to take their possessions down a river. They were like rafts with sides. Make one raft design and one keelboat design similar to those illustrated here. Test each model to see how many weights it can hold before sinking.

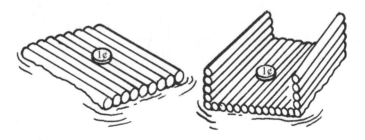

Water Displacement

The heavier a boat becomes, the more water it displaces (moves aside) as it floats in the water. You can determine exactly how much water each of your boats displaces.

1. Place a clear widemouthed plastic cup in a plastic bowl or small tray.
2. Fill the cup with water exactly even with the lip of the cup.
3. Place your aluminum barge on the water in the full cup.
4. Put as many weights in the aluminum barge as you can without sinking it.
5. Use a small measuring cup to determine how much water was displaced.
6. Test each of your designs in the same way and compare your results. Determine which design displaced the most water.

Boats and Barges *(cont.)*

Ships Ahoy

Examine the ships illustrated here. Choose one of these designs to build a model. Try to include all of the design features shown. The materials you use may include craft sticks, toothpicks, straws, clay, Styrofoam trays and cups, plastic bottles, plastic and paper milk cartons, crayons, tape, glue, rubber bands, aluminum foil, cardboard, pipe cleaners, wire, and other materials of your own choosing.

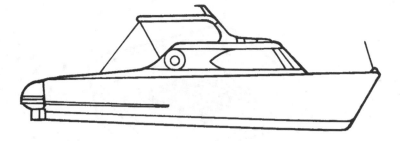

Outboard Cruiser

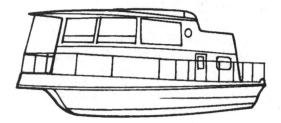

Houseboat

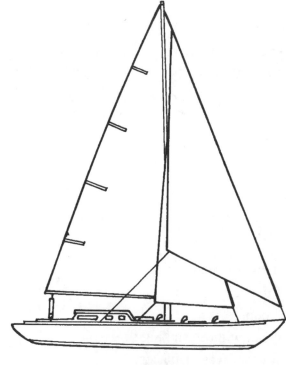

Sloop

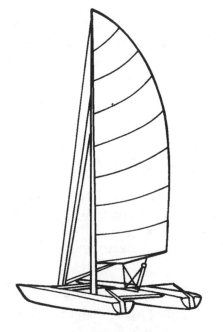

Catamaran

Boats and Barges *(cont.)*

Become the Design Engineer

Create your own ship design and build it from the materials of your choice. Decide what kind of ship you want it to be and what you want the ship to do. You may choose to modify one of the designs on the preceding page or make one entirely of your own imagination.

Tips and Techniques

Consider these tips while building your model ship.

1. Balance the weight of the boat itself from side to side and front to back.
2. A wide, flat area distributes the weight and places more water under the boat so that a heavier load can be carried.
3. Use light, strong, waterproof materials.
4. Higher sides allow the ship to hold more weight and ride lower in the water without sinking.
5. Allow glue to dry before putting the ship into the water.
6. Try using a balloon, a toy motor, sails, a rubber band and stick paddle, or other materials to provide propulsion.
7. Details matter. Make it look good and work well.

The Regatta

Evaluate the quality of each of your ships by testing them on the water. This will enable you to assess how much you have learned about buoyancy.

1. Fill a toddler's pool or large tray with water.
2. Use a pen to mark the water line on the side of the boat when it is empty.
3. Tape packs of 10 pennies together.
4. Place as many of these 10-penny packs in each ship as you can without sinking it. Mark the water line on the loaded ship with a pen.
5. Record how heavy a load the ship carried.
6. Test any propulsion devices such as sails, a motor, or a paddle to see if the ship will move.
7. Decide how you could have improved your boat.

Whirlybirds

Concepts: *gravity, air resistance, and slipstreaming*

Materials: paper, scissors, small paper clips, large paper clips, index cards, manila folder, markers or crayons

Optional: tagboard, other paper of various thicknesses

Whirlybird

Make the simple whirlybird design illustrated here.

1. Cut along the dotted lines.
2. Fold along the dark lines.
3. Add one paper clip to the fuselage.
4. Fold one rotor back. Fold the other rotor forward.
5. Hold the whirlybird by the top of the rotors as high off the ground as you can reach.
6. Release the model. Observe how the whirlybird falls. Do several trials.
7. Use a marker or crayon to color one rotor. Drop the whirlybird and use the colored rotor as an aid in counting how many times the rotors turn before it lands.
8. Do several trials and keep a record of your results. Make a graph to compare your results.

The Twister

You can make a model that twirls faster by using a smaller design. Reduce the design illustrated and repeat the directions above.

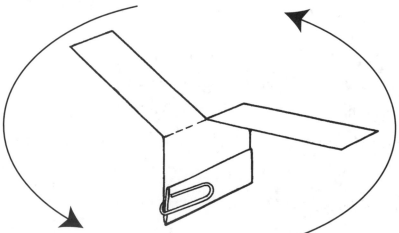

Fuselage

Rotor   Rotor

Whirlybirds *(cont.)*

You can change the flight characteristics of your models by modifying the rotors or the fuselage. Take your whirlybird model and try the modifications described below.

1. Reverse the folds on your model. How does this affect the direction?
2. Twist each rotor in a different direction. How does this affect the flight?
3. Fold the rotor over to create a triangular shape at the tip of each rotor. Test this version of your model.
4. Cut away part of each rotor and test this version.
5. Fold the model in an accordion pattern and then test it.
6. Add some paper to each rotor to increase the width or the weight of the rotor. Test this model.
7. Cut out an outline of a pilot about one inch (2.54 cm) tall and tape the pilot to the fuselage. Test this model.

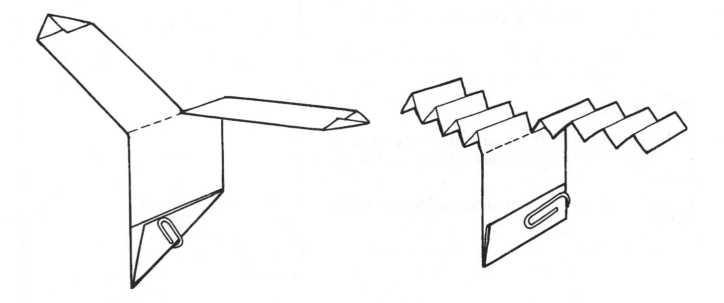

Variations

- Choose one of the previous models to make out of an index card, a manila folder, or a different kind of paper. Compare your results.
- Try the same material with another design.
- Use colors or markers to decorate the rotors and the body of the models. Notice what happens to the colors when the whirlybirds are dropped.
- Try different line designs, geometric shapes, or patterns on the rotors. Observe what happens to the appearance of the designs when the model is falling.

Whirlybirds *(cont.)*

The Wide Body

1. Copy and cut out the model illustrated here.
2. Notice that the shape and folding pattern are different. Fold one rotor forward and one rotor backward as before.
3. Hold the model by the rotors and drop it. Observe the results.
4. Color one rotor. Drop the model as you did before and count the number of twirls before it lands.
5. Add one small paper clip to the fuselage and test the model again. Count the number of twirls before it lands.
6. Add a second paper clip and count the twirls again.
7. Add a third paper clip and record the number of twirls.

   • How many paper clips can you add before it drops straight without twirling?

The Thin Body

Build a thin version of the illustration (no more than 2" or 5 cm wide). Fold the rotors as before and test your model.

Color one rotor and count how many twirls occur before it lands.

Add one small paper clip to the fuselage and test the model again. Count the number of twirls before it lands.

Add a second paper clip and count the twirls again. Add a third paper clip and count the twirls again.

• How many paper clips can you add before it drops straight without twirling?

Variations

• Hold the wide-body model in one hand and the thin model in the other.
• Hold the models by the rotors as high as you can and drop them at the same time.
• Determine which model twirls faster.
• Determine which model falls faster.
• Test each model in the same way with one, two, and three paper clips on the fuselage.
• Record your results on a chart.

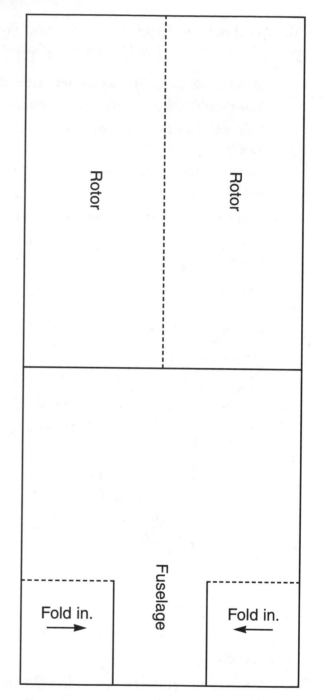

Whirlybirds *(cont.)*

Three Rotors

1. Copy and cut out the model pictured here. Be sure to fold the rotors in opposite directions.
2. Test fly your three-rotor model. You may have to try several times before you get a successful flight.
3. Add a paper clip to the model and try it. Add a second and a third paper clip. Will the model work?
4. Design your own three-rotor model. Use a different length of paper, a different pattern, or different measurements.
5. Test fly it and compare it to the first three-rotor model.
6. Make your model out of tagboard and test your results.

Four Rotors (and More)

Create your own design for a four-rotor model. Remember to fold each rotor the opposite direction from the ones next to it. Test fly your model. It may take several trials before it will twirl. Try adding small paper clips to improve the flight. Use different materials, such as thicker paper, an index card, or tagboard to get a more successful model. Try a wider version or a shorter one. Try a much larger one or a very tiny model.

The Drop Contest

Create at least five of your own models of the whirlybird.

Consider these factors when you make your design:

- shape—wide or narrow, long or short
- number of rotors—two, three, four, or more
- fuselage design—shape of the fold, load it might carry
- weight—number of paper clips
- rotors—folded, twisted, bent, curved, or cut away

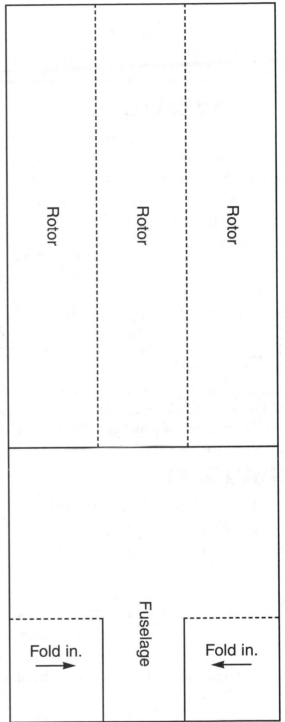

Test each of your models several times.

Choose two models to drop in a classroom demonstration with your classmates. You may make your choice using any of the following criteria:

- Most Interesting
- Most Unusual
- Fastest Twirler
- Best Looking
- Slowest Fall
- Heaviest Load

Flying Circus

Concepts: *properties of flight*
Materials: 8.5" x 11" (21 cm x 28 cm) paper, small paper clips, glue, tape, ruler

The Loop de Loop

1. Cut a piece of paper two inches wide and eight inches long (5 cm x 20 cm). Fold this paper into a loop and tape it around one end of a straw.

2. Cut a second piece of paper one inch wide (2.54 cm) and six inches (15 cm) long. Fold this paper into a loop and tape it around the other end of the straw.

3. Hold the Loop de Loop by the end with the larger loop and gently flip the model into the air.

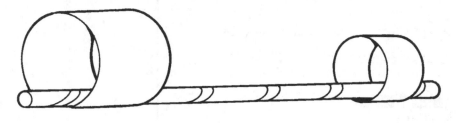

More Loops

Make your own loop design. Try larger loops, smaller ones, three or four loops on a straw, and loops made of different materials. Try adding two or three small paper clips to the front of the first loop. Use different types of paper and different straw sizes. Demonstrate your best design for the class.

Flying Cones

1. Fold a sheet of paper 1½ inches (3.8 cm) down from the top.

2. Fold it over two more times.

3. Fold this set of layers in half so that there are eight folded layers.

4. Fold one corner from the opposite end of the paper along the center in a triangle shape.

5. Do the same with the other corner of the paper.

6. Curl one side of the folded paper around to make a circle and tuck one side into the other. Tape in place.

7. Place a small paper clip over the taped area.

8. Hold the model cupped in your hand and launch it with a flick of the wrist.

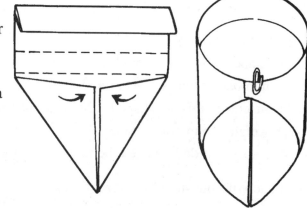

Design and fly your own cones. Use different folding techniques. Use different launching techniques. Compare your designs with those of your classmates.

Flying Circus *(cont.)*

Study the designs illustrated on these pages. Fold each one in the described sequence.

The V Flyer

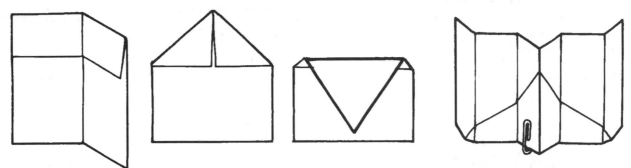

1. Fold the paper three inches (8 cm) down from the top and then fold it in half down the middle.
2. Bring each corner down to the center and fold the triangle along the center line.
3. Fold the triangular tip of the paper down to one inch (2.54 cm) from the bottom of the paper. Fold the plane along the center line again.
4. Measure one inch (2.54 cm) from the center fold in each direction and fold along these lines to create the fuselage.
5. Measure one inch (2.54 cm) from each edge of the paper and fold each edge up to create the rudders.
6. The weight of a paper plane needs to be in the nose. Add one or two small paper clips to some part of the nose to get better flight characteristics. Launch the plane with a gentle flip of the wrist. If you throw too hard, the plane will usually just fall.

The Swept-Back Wing

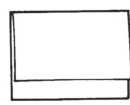 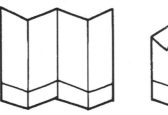 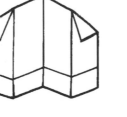 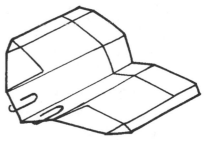

1. Fold the paper down to one inch (2.54 cm) from the bottom. Then fold it in half down the middle.
2. Measure 1½ inches (3.8 cm) from the center fold in each direction and fold along these lines to create the fuselage.
3. Bring each corner down to the upper fold of the fuselage and fold the triangle along the upper fold. Tape each fold in place.
4. Measure ½ inch (1.3 cm) from each edge of the paper and fold each edge down to create the rudders.
5. Attach small paper clips along the front edge of the plane as shown.

Flying Circus *(cont.)*

The Twirler

1. Fold the paper two inches (5 cm) down from the top. Fold the paper again two more inches from the top.
2. Fold the paper in half down the middle.
3. Measure 1½ inches (3.8 cm) from the center fold in each direction and fold along these lines to create the fuselage.
4. Bring each top corner down to the center fold of the fuselage about two inches (5 cm) from the nose and fold the triangle.
5. Fold along the fuselage lines again.
6. Measure ¾ inch (2 cm) from each edge of the paper and fold each edge up to create the rudders.
7. Place one small paper clip on the nose to keep the sides of the fuselage together and provide weight in the nose.

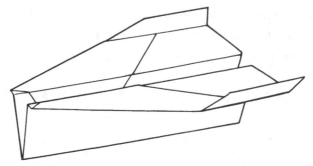

The Wide Glider

- Try more paper clips.
- Launch the model with a harder throw or a gentler flick of the wrist.
- Fold the rudders down and launch it that way.

The Wide Glider

1. Fold the paper in half down the middle.
2. Bring each corner down to the center and fold the triangle along the center line.
3. Fold the tip of the triangle two inches (5 cm) down so that the tip is along the fold line of the triangles.
4. Fold the top of the paper two more inches and crease it again.
5. Fold the paper in half along the crease again.
6. Measure three inches (8 cm) out from the center fold in each direction and fold down along these lines to create the wings. There is no real fuselage.
7. The edges serve as rudders.

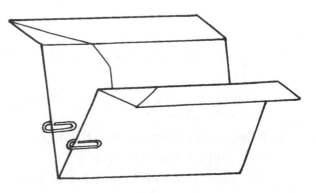

Flying Circus *(cont.)*

Design Your Own

Design your own version of a paper plane. Keep these ideas in mind as you work.

- The paper plane will usually fly better if the weight is in the nose.
- Symmetrical folding helps keep the plane evenly balanced.
- Making the folds sharp with the help of scissors or a ruler will often improve the flight characteristics.
- The plane should have an obvious fuselage and rudder.
- Launch the plane gently rather than with force.

Military Jet   **Stealth Bomber**   **Jet Airliner**

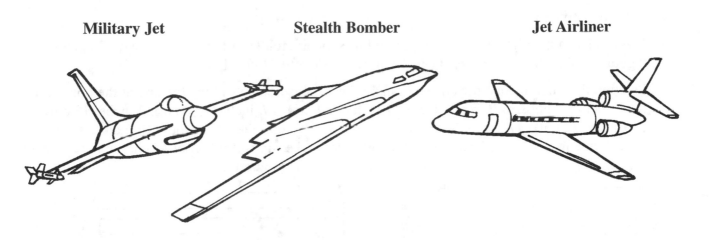

Indoor Air Circus

Pick your best model or two from all of the paper planes you have made for a flying contest in the room or in a cafeteria. Use a clearly designated flying area where no one will get hit by a plane.

There should be four categories of competition:

- Duration—Which plane stayed in the air the longest?
- Distance—Which plane flew the farthest?
- Height—Which plane went the highest?
- Loops and Turns—Which plane made the most interesting loops or turns in the air?

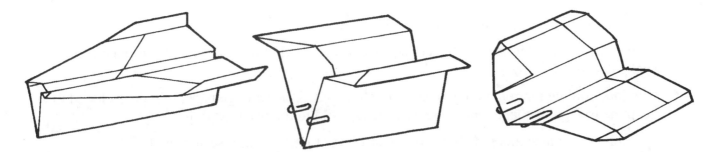

Gleaming Gliders

Concepts: *properties of flight*
Materials: manila folders or tagboard, large paper clips, glue, tape, construction paper

Making the Fuselage

Making the fuselage or shaft of the glider is the most important and difficult part of the project.

The same shaft can be used for all of the gliders in this unit. It is rugged, durable, and reinforced so that it does not bend easily.

Follow these instructions exactly:

1. Use a ruler to measure from the center fold of a manila folder or the straight edge of a piece of tagboard. The shaft should be 11 to 12 inches (28 cm to 31 cm) long.

2. Position the ruler against the edge and mark these measurements at the top and at the bottom of the folder or tagboard: $\frac{1}{2}$ inch (.6 cm), 1 inch (2.54 cm), $1\frac{1}{2}$ inches (3.8 cm), 2 inches (5 cm), $2\frac{3}{4}$ inches (7 cm), $3\frac{1}{2}$ inches (9.3 cm), $4\frac{1}{4}$ inches (10.6 cm) and $5\frac{1}{4}$ inches (13.6 cm). (The measurements get larger because folding this paper takes up space.) Your teacher may have made a paper copy of these measurements which you can use as a model.

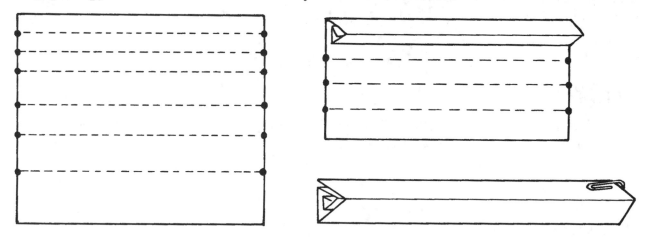

3. Use a ruler to draw precise, straight lines connecting the dots for each measurement.

4. Go over the pencil lines with the edge of a ruler. This scores the lines and makes it easier to get a sharp fold.

5. Fold along the lines and crease them sharply.

6. Start from the smaller, half-inch increments and fold the first three layers into the shape of a triangular prism.

7. Continue folding the remaining layers over the prism. Place a large paper clip on each end to keep the triangular shape while you glue the last fold to the one next to it.

8. Use cellophane tape along the edge of the last layer to get a firmly sealed shaft.

Gleaming Gliders *(cont.)*

The Equilateral Flyer

All of the wings and rudders on this glider are made from equilateral (equal-sided) triangles.

1. Cut out the wing and rudder patterns shown on this page or use a compass and ruler to make the following features:
    a. an 8-inch (20 cm) base front wing
    b. a 7-inch (18 cm) overlapping front wing
    c. a 4-inch (10 cm) rear wing
    d. rear rudders, each 3 inches (8 cm) per side
2. Make the shaft using the instructions detailed on page 26.
3. Line up the front wing one inch (2.54 cm) from the tip of the shaft and align the wing so that it is evenly balanced left and right of the shaft. Glue it to the shaft and tape it to reinforce the glue.
4. Center the smaller overlapping front wing on top of the eight-inch (20 cm) base. Glue this to the larger base.
5. Place the four-inch (10 cm) rear wing against the rear of the shaft. Align the wing so that it is evenly balanced. Glue it to the shaft and tape it for better support.
6. Fold each rudder piece ½ inch (1.3 cm) from one side of the triangle. Align the two rudder pieces on the rear wing against the rear of the shaft.
7. Glue each rudder along this ½ fold to the rear wing. Tape them for better adhesion. Glue the rudders together.
8. Put at least four large paper clips on the nose of the glider.

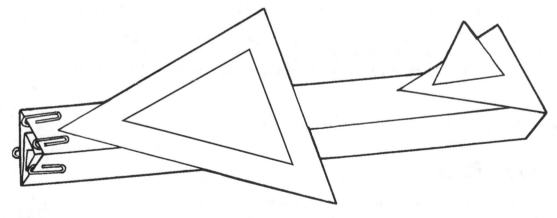

Outdoor Flying

Flying the gliders outdoors depends on weather conditions. It usually is more difficult and requires more effort to get a successful flight. You will always need to have more weight in the nose of the plane. You may need to tape two to four large paper clips along the front of the wing. You may want to tape a pencil inside the shaft to get more weight and durability. Usually you will want to launch the glider into the wind. Try launching it away from the wind. Try launching it across wind currents. Look for adjustments to make the glider fly better. Does your glider do loops? How far does the glider go?

Gleaming Gliders *(cont.)*

The Isosceles Fighter

The single wing on this glider is an isosceles triangle with a base of eight inches (20 cm) and two sides 10½ inches (26.7 cm) long.

1. Cut out the wing and rudder patterns shown on this page or use a compass and ruler to make them.
2. Make the shaft using the instructions on page 26.
3. Line up the wing along the rear of the shaft and align the wing so that it is evenly balanced left and right of the shaft. Glue it to the shaft and tape it to reinforce the glue.
4. Each rudder piece has a six-inch (15 cm) base and two four-inch (10 cm) sides. Fold each rudder piece one inch (2.54 cm) from one four-inch (10 cm) side of the triangle (leaving 3" to stand upright). Align the two rudder pieces on the rear wing against the rear of the shaft.
5. Glue each rudder along this one-inch (2.54 cm) fold to the rear wing. Tape them for better adhesion. Glue the rudders together.
6. Put at least four large paper clips on the nose of the glider.

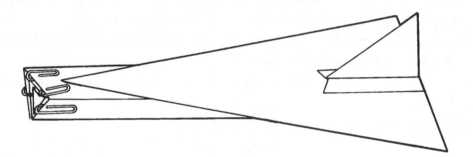

When launching the glider outdoors, add more
paper clips to the nose and try taping two paper clips to the upper edge of the wing.

Launch the glider into the wind.

Try launching it away from the wind or across the wind currents.

The Passenger Plane

1. Use a compass and ruler to make these features:
   a. front wing—11" (28 cm) base, 3" (8 cm) sides, 4½" (11.3 cm) slanting front, and 3" (8 cm) center front
   b. bottom reinforcing strap along the front wing—11" x 2" (28x5 cm)
   c. top reinforcing strap along the front wing—11" x 2" (28x5 cm)
   d. rear wing—6" (15 cm) base , 2" (5 cm) sides, 2 ¼" (5.6 cm) slanting front, and 2" (5 cm) center front.
   e. rudder—4" (10 cm) base, 1 ½" (3.8 cm) sides, 1 ½" (3.8 cm) slanting front, 1" (2.54 cm center front.

Gleaming Gliders *(cont.)*

The Passenger Plane *(cont.)*

2. Make the shaft using the instructions detailed on page 26.
3. Line up the front wing 1½ inches (3.8 cm) from the tip of the shaft and align the wing so that it is evenly balanced left and right of the shaft. Glue it to the shaft and tape it to reinforce the glue.
4. Glue the bottom reinforcing strap to the bottom edge of the front wing. These straps provide stability and provide better lift for the front wing.
5. Glue the top reinforcing strap to the bottom edge of the first reinforcing strap. These straps provide stability and provide better lift for the front wing.
6. Place the rear wing against the rear of the shaft. Align the wing so that it is evenly balanced. Glue it to the shaft and tape it for better support.
7. Fold the rudder piece on both sides along the center inch. Center the rudder on the rear wing against the rear of the shaft.
8. Glue the rudder along this one-inch (2.54 cm) base to the rear wing. Tape it down for better adhesion. Glue and tape the rudder tips together.
9. Put at least four large paper clips on the nose of the glider.

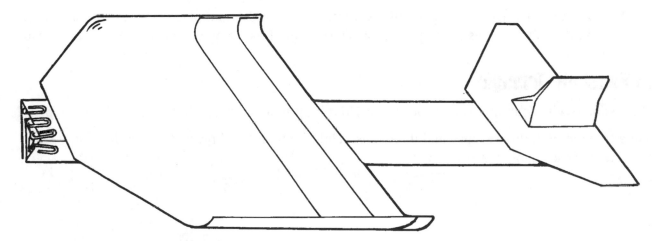

Create Your Own Design

Create your own glider design using manila folder or tagboard. Carefully design your wings to stay in the air once launched. Consider using reinforcing straps so that the wing is not as floppy. Use several large paper clips to get better thrust and provide weight in the nose of the glider. Design a rudder that allows your glider to stay evenly balanced in the air. Participate in a flying contest, either indoors or outdoors. Use a clearly designated flying area where no one will get hit by a glider.

There should be four categories of competition:

- Duration—Which glider stayed in the air the longest?
- Distance—Which glider flew the farthest?
- Height—Which glider went the highest?
- Loops and Turns—Which glider made the most interesting loops or turns in the air?

Bold Bridges

Concept: *strength of geometric shapes*
Materials: straws, straight pins, scissors, fishing line, pennies, small Styrofoam tray
Optional: large paper clips, string

The Basic Bridge

1. Use straws and straight pins to construct a flat bridge between two desks like the bridge pictured here. It should be constructed with squares and be three feet (91 cm) long. It should extend onto each desk about the length of one square.

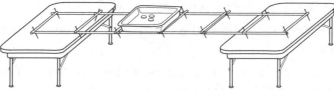

2. Press your hand on the bridge. Push on one side and then the other. Notice how easily the bridge bends and the sides slide toward each other.

3. Place a small, flat Styrofoam plate on the center of the bridge and place pennies (or large paper clips) in the tray. Add as many pennies as you can until the bridge collapses. Record the result.

The Superior Triangle

Make a square with four straws and four pins. Hold it upright and press down on it. What happens?

Make a triangle with three straws and three pins. Hold it upright and press down on it. Can you determine that the triangle is stronger?

Remove and replace any broken straws in your bridge. Add diagonal reinforcements as shown in the illustration. You can make the diagonal straws long enough by slitting the end of one straw with scissors and fitting the slit end inside another straw or by pinning two straws together. Pin the diagonal reinforcements at the four corners of the square and in the middle. This creates four triangles within each square.

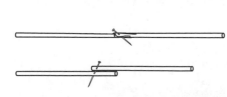 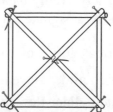

Place the Styrofoam plate on the center of the bridge again and add pennies. Add as many as you can until the bridge collapses. How many more pennies did the bridge hold this time? Record the result.

Bold Bridges *(cont.)*

Beam It Up

Build one cube made of straws on each side of the bridge. Use diagonal reinforcements on all faces of each cube. Test the strength of this beam bridge with the weights.

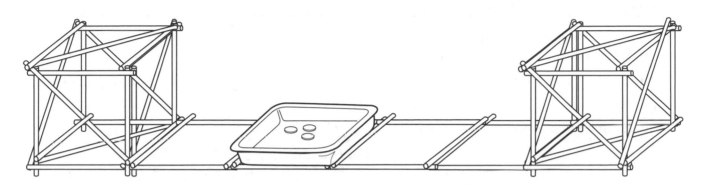

Use squares to build up each side of the bridge. Connect the tops of the squares with straws so that a series of cubes are formed.

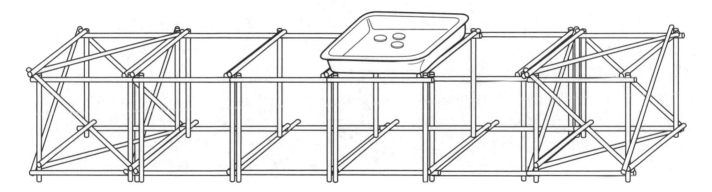

Place the small Styrofoam tray on the center of the bridge as before. Place as many pennies as you can on the tray. Determine how many pennies the bridge will hold before it collapses.

Building a Better Beam Bridge

1. Replace any broken or damaged straws in your bridge.
2. Insert diagonal reinforcements along the sides of your bridge just as you did on the base.
3. Use the small Styrofoam tray at the center of the bridge and pennies to test how much your bridge will hold before falling.
4. Add the same type of reinforcement along the top of your bridge and retest it to determine how much weight it will now hold.
5. Record your final total and make a graph to illustrate the number of weights held by the structures each of your classmates made.

Bold Bridges *(cont.)*

An Arch Bridge

In an arch bridge, the curve of the arch shifts the weight to the supports at each end.

1. Thread about four or five straws firmly together with the ends slit and inserted into the next straw so that you have one long "straw" about 35 inches (88 cm) long.

2. Bend this long straw into an arch shape and pin it to the support towers and the underside of the bridge as shown in the illustration.

3. Make a second long "straw" in the same way and pin it to the other side of the supports and the bridge.

4. Make two more shorter arches in the same way.

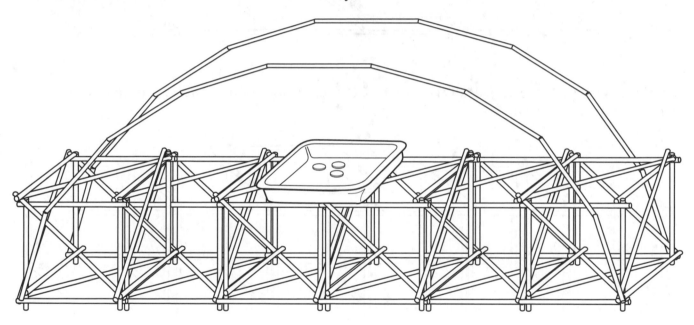

5. Use reinforcing straws to attach each long, curved "straw" to the structure of the bridge as shown in the illustration.

6. Use the tray of pennies to test the strength of your bridge. Remember to place them in the center of the bridge.

7. Do several trials and replace any broken straws. Record your best trial.

8. Make a graph or chart to record the results for your class. Compare the bridges to see why some held more weight than others.

Suspension Bridge

In a suspension bridge, the suspending cables exert an upward force which, along with the towers, supports the weight. Use fishing line (or string), straws, and pins to make a bridge like the Golden Gate on page 33. Use a pin to make in the upright straws a hole large enough to thread the fishing line cable through the top of each straw.

Bold Bridges *(cont.)*

Famous Bridges

Several famous bridges or types of bridges are illustrated below. Choose one of these bridges to reproduce, using your straws, pins, and other materials. Make your model as accurate as possible.

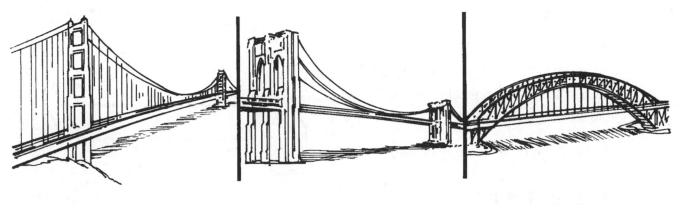

Golden Gate Bridge   **Brooklyn Bridge**   **Sydney Harbor**

Build Your Own Bridge

In the space shown here, design a bridge that you can build out of pins, straws, and fishing line, if needed. Demonstrate what you have learned about bridges by using one or several features of bridge design.

Test Your Bridge Model

Compare your results with the penny roll weights held by your other bridge models.

The Best Bubble Maker

Concept: *properties of soap (detergent) film*

Materials: string or thin twine, insulated wire, straws, dish soap (detergent), water, vegetable oil

---

Bubble Chemistry

Use this formula to make a strong bubble solution:

- 20 ounces (600 mL) of dish detergent (Dawn, Joy)
- 6 ounces (180 mL) of vegetable oil
- 2 gallons (7.6 L) of water

Stir the solution thoroughly in a tray or tub.

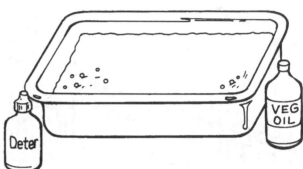

The Two-Handle Frame

Cut a piece of string or thin twine about 30 inches (76 cm) long. Thread the string through the two straws and tie the ends of the string together.

Using the two straws as handles, dip the frame into the bubble solution and see how large a bubble you can lift out of the solution.

Twist the frame to create two triangles. Can you lift two bubbles out of the solution with this frame?

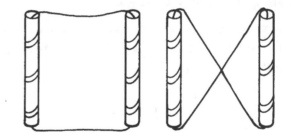

The Circle Frame

1. Cut a piece of string about 36 inches (91 cm) long.
2. Thread it through five straws.
3. Slit the ends of each straw so that each straw fits into the ends of the straw on each side of it.
4. Tie the string tightly so that the straws and string form a circle.

Dip this frame into the solution and observe the results as you lift the bubbles out of the solution.

Geometric Frames

Use string and straws to create a square frame, an equilateral triangular frame, and a rectangular bubble maker.

Dip these frames into the solution and observe your results. Why do you think that the bubbles are always spherical?

The Best Bubble Maker *(cont.)*

More Geometric Frames

Twist thin, insulated wire into several of the shapes illustrated here.

Try these shapes in your bubble formula. Observe how the bubbles form. Can you get any long bubbles using some of these frames? Thread wire through short pieces of cut straws to create the plane geometric figures illustrated here.

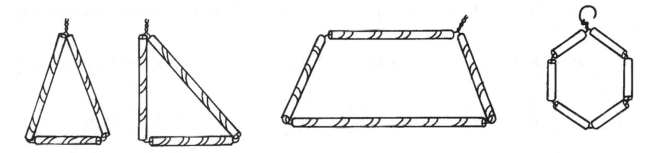

Can you make a heptagon (7 sides), a decagon (10 sides), and a dodecagon (12 sides)?

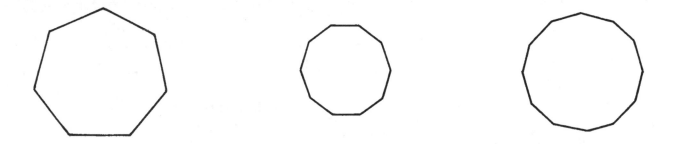

- How do these figures work with the bubble solution?
- Try putting a dry finger through the soapy film on one of the figures.
- Try putting a wet finger through the film.
- Blow gently on the soapy film in the faces of the geometric figures.
- Gently sweep the figure through the air.
- Try making a long bubble by slowly pulling the figure through the air or blowing on it.
- Do some figures work better than others?

The Best Bubble Maker *(cont.)*

Soapy Prisms

Use thin insulated wire and straws to make the geometric prisms illustrated on this page.

Cut the straws the same size for the shapes that have equal-sided edges.

You may need to thread more than one wire through some straws to make the figures.

The Cube (Hexahedron)

Follow these directions for the cube (hexahedron):

1. Thread one wire through four straws of equal length and twist it tight to make a square.
2. Use the same wire if any remains or another wire to thread through three more straws of equal length to add one side of the cube.
3. Twist this wire onto the bottom square.
4. Thread another wire through three more straws of equal length to add the other side of the cube.
5. Thread a wire through one straw and connect it to both ends of the cube. Connect the remaining straw side in the same way.

Cube (Hexahedron)

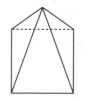

Triangular Prism

Triangular Pyramid

Square Pyramid

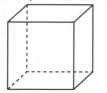

Rectangular Prism

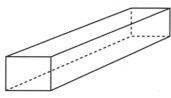

Octahedron

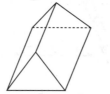

Icosahedron

Dodecahedron

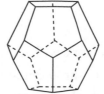

When you try these figures in the soapy solution, note how the soap film arranges itself in each prism. Look for lines and points within each prism.

Try putting a dry finger through one of the faces. Try putting a wet finger through a face.

Blow gently on the soapy film in the faces.

Gently sweep the figure through the air.

The Best Bubble Maker *(cont.)*

Twirling Bubbles

1. Make a rectangular frame and connect a rubber band to each side of the frame.
2. Wind up the rubber bands by twisting the figure until the rubber bands are tight.
3. Dip the wound-up frame into the solution.
4. Remove the frame from the solution and pull on the rubber bands to make the frame twist around rapidly.

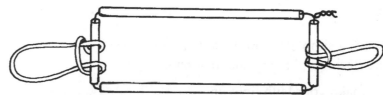

Connect a rubber band to each side of an octahedron or another prism you made. Wind up the figure with the rubber bands. Insert the figure into the solution. Bring the figure out of the soapy solution and pull on the rubber bands to untwist the figure. Are the bubbles formed as well as before? Did you get one or many bubbles?

Ultra Bubbles

Safety Note: Never touch any electrical equipment with wet hands!

Try using a hair dryer or a fan with some of the figures you have made.

Hook the fan or dryer a safe distance from the bubble solution. It could be connected inside with the fan or dryer sitting outside on a table well away from the water.

Dip your fingers into the solution and hold them in front of the fan or blowers.

What results did you get?

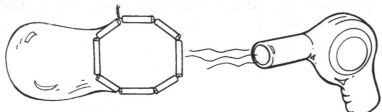

Create your own designs for a bubble frame. Be creative. Try different materials such as hangers or long pieces of yarn.

- Try making bubbles with your hand alone. Use really different shapes.
- What is the largest bubble you can make?
- What is the longest bubble you can make?
- Design your own soapy formula using your own combination of soap, water, and/or other ingredients.
- Can you make better bubbles, bigger bubbles, or bubbles which last longer?
- Demonstrate your bubble frames and bubble formula to your classmates.

Circuit Cities

Concepts: *electricity and circuits*

Materials: flashlight batteries, bulbs, insulated bell wire, rough sandpaper, bulb holders (sockets), large paper clips, rubber bands

Optional: battery holders

Simple Circuits

The illustration below shows a simple circuit made with one piece of insulated bell wire, one flashlight battery, and one bulb.

Follow these directions to make your bulb light up.

1. Use a small square of rough sandpaper to strip the insulation off each end of the wire. Leave about one inch (2.54 cm) of bare wire on each end.

2. The insulation strips best if you place the end of the wire inside the folded sandpaper and then squeeze, twist, and pull the sandpaper against the wire.

3. Hold one end of the bare wire against the bottom or negative pole of the battery.

4. Hold the base of the bulb against the top or positive pole of the battery.

5. Touch the other bare end of the wire against the metal side of the bulb.

6. The bulb should light.

   • Try to find three other ways to light the bulb using only the battery, bulb, and wire. Think upside down. Think backwards.

   • Draw a picture of each way you got the bulb to light.

Using Sockets

Add a bulb holder or socket to your circuit. Screw the bulb gently but firmly into the holder. Make sure the bottom of the bulb is touching the bottom metal piece of the socket. Attach one bare end of one wire to one clip on the socket. Press down on the clip, and the wire will feed through the "eye" of the socket.

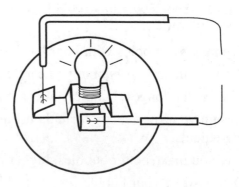

Use the sandpaper to strip the ends of one more piece of insulated wire and attach one bare end of that wire to the other clip in the socket.

Circuit Cities *(cont.)*

Adding the Battery Holder

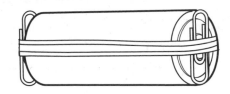

1. Double two average size rubber bands so that there are four layers and wrap them over a C or D cell battery from end to end.

2. Insert one large paper clip between the rubber band layers and the metal positive pole at the top of the battery. Be sure the paper clip is firmly held against the metal.

3. Insert another large paper clip between the rubber band layers and the metal negative pole at the bottom of the battery. Be sure the paper clip is firmly held against the metal.

Switched On

1. Connect the unattached end of one wire leading from the socket to the paper clip on one pole of the battery.

2. Connect one bare end of the second wire to the other paper clip on the other pole of the battery.

3. Make sure that each wire is securely attached to the paper clip. It is best if the wire and paper clip are both held against the pole by the rubber band.

4. Wrap another large paper clip around the wire extending from the battery.

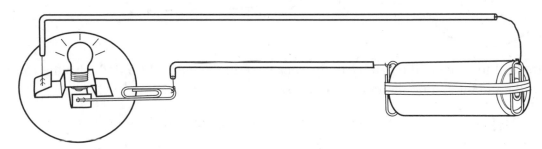

5. Touch the paper clip to the empty side of the socket. The bulb should light because there is a complete circuit running from the source of power, the battery, along the wire to the bulb and back to the battery again.

6. When the paper clip is removed from the empty socket clip, the circuit is broken and electricity cannot flow in an unbroken stream or current.

Variations

- Are there any ways you can change the arrangement of the circuit and still get the bulb to go on and off?
- Can the paper clip switch extend from the socket instead of the battery?
- Can you tap the paper clip switch against a wire of the battery?
- Try several combinations.

Circuit Cities *(cont.)*

Super Circuits

1. Start with the basic circuit you used on the last page. Use another wire with the ends stripped bare to connect the socket to a pair of metal scissors as shown in the illustration.

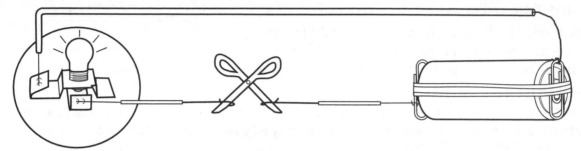

2. Arrange the scissors in another part of the circuit. Can you still make the bulb light?

3. Fold a strip of aluminum foil into a long thin band of foil.

4. Use the foil to connect the scissors to the battery as shown here. Does the light still go on? Why?

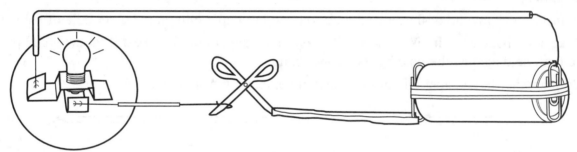

5. Use the foil to connect the battery to the socket. Will the bulb still light? Use the foil in another part of the circuit so that the bulb still lights.

Electric Coins

1. Find one or two coins to add to your circuit. Try the arrangement shown below.

2. Arrange one or more of your coins in another part of the circuit so that the bulb still lights.

3. Draw a sketch showing your circuit design with the coins.

4. Do some coins work better than others? Why?

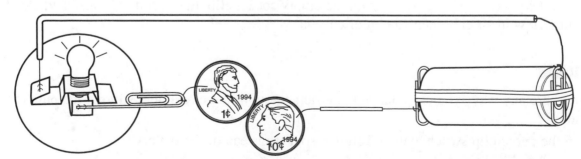

5. Arrange all of your materials in three different circuit patterns that work. Sketch each pattern.

Circuit Cities (cont.)

Your Name in Lights

1. Cut long strips of aluminum foil. Use the strips to spell your name in foil on a large sheet of construction paper or on a folder.

2. Bend the strips and arrange them so that each letter of your name is connected.

3. Carefully use clear tape along the edges of the foil to attach the strips to the paper or folder. Leave a strip of untaped foil along the center of every letter.

4. Connect one wire from the battery holder to the strips of foil. Place the bare end securely under and against the foil as shown in the illustration.

5. Connect the second wire from the battery to a large paper clip. Make sure the bare end of the wire is wrapped several times around the clip. Insert the bulb into the open end of the clip.

6. Hold the paper clip and bulb on the foil and trace the name. The bulb should remain lit as long as it travels over the foil which is not covered with tape.

7. Find two other arrangements using the socket, battery, and bulb that will keep the bulb lit.

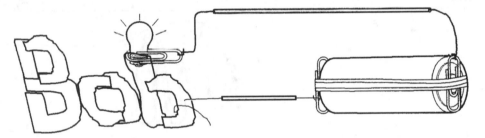

Circuit Cities

1. Create an outline of a city street somewhat like the one illustrated below. Use your own town or make up a city arrangement of your own.

2. Cut long strips of foil and use them to make the road in your city. Carefully tape them down so that the center of the road is not covered with tape and leaves a clear trail for the bulb to follow.

3. Use the battery and bulb arrangement you used with your name or one of the others you discovered to follow the road along your city as you followed the name above.

- Can you turn the paper clip/bulb holder into a model car using small pieces of paper and other materials?

4. Add a long road around the outside of your city.

5. Create a more complicated city with detours, roadblocks, dead ends, and other complications.

Centripetal Spinners

Concepts: *centripetal force*

Materials: nylon fishline, large paper clips, small paper clips, small cup, modeling clay, water, tape

Optional: plastic tubing, washers, other materials

The Basic Spinner

1. Cut a piece of fishline about 12 inches (30 cm) long.
2. Tie one end of the line securely to a small paper clip.
3. Cut a straw in half and feed the fishline through one of the halves.
4. Tie four large paper clips to the remaining end of the line as shown in the illustration.

5. Hold the end with the large paper clips in one hand and gently rotate the straw with the other hand. The spinner should lift the large paper clips off your hand and pull them toward the lower end of the straw.

Variations

- Try spinning the model as slowly as you can without having the little paper clip pulled down against the top of the straw.
- Try spinning the model as fast as you can without stopping the motion of the spinner.
- Get the model spinning and then turn the straw horizontally and try spinning it with the model in this position.

- Add one more large paper clip to the ones already there. Spin the model again.

- Keep adding another large paper clip to the model and rotating the spinner until it will no longer work.

- How many large paper clips can you use and still keep the model spinning?

Centripetal Spinners *(cont.)*

The Extra Long Spinner

1. Cut a piece of fishline about two feet (61 cm) long and tie one end of the line securely to a small paper clip.
2. Cut a straw in half and feed the fishline through one of the halves. Slit the other half straw with scissors and slip this half straw over the first one to make a stronger tube. Tape it in place.
3. Tie four large paper clips to the remaining end of the line as you did with the first model.

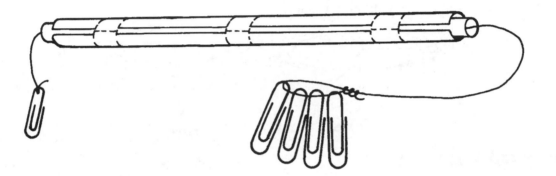

4. Hold the end with the large paper clips in one hand as you did before and rotate the straw with the other hand.

Can you get the longer spinner to lift the large paper clips off your hand?

- Try spinning the model as slowly as you can without having the little paper clip pulled against the top of the straw.
- Try spinning the model as fast as you can without stopping the motion of the spinner.
- Try spinning the model in several different directions (horizontally, at a 45° angle, and at several different angles).
- Which directions can you hold it and get the model to work?

- Keep adding large paper clips to the model and rotating the spinner until it will no longer work.
- How many large paper clips can you use and still keep the model spinning?

Centripetal Spinners *(cont.)*

Longtime Spinners

- Use either of the two models you have made to determine how long you can spin the model before it stops.
- Time yourself with a watch.
- Try a spin-off with a classmate to see which of you can spin the model the longest.
- Try spinning two models at one time with one in each hand.
- Can you spin them both?
- Can you change directions with either hand?

Planetary Spinners

1. Cut a piece of fishline about 18 inches (46 cm) long.
2. Bend open a small paper clip so that it has a mouth about 90° and tie the bent paper clip to one end of the fishline.
3. Press about ½ ounce (14 g) of modeling clay around the bent paper clip to form a sphere about the size of a Ping-Pong ball.
4. Cut a straw in half and feed the fishline through one of the halves. Slit the other half straw with scissors and slip this half straw over the first one to make a stronger tube. Tape it in place.
5. Bend a second small paper clip to a 90° angle as you did before and tie it to the remaining end of the fishline.
6. Press about one ounce (28 g) of modeling clay around the bent paper clip to form a sphere about the size of a tennis ball.

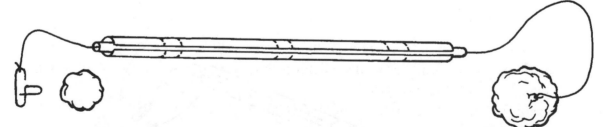

The smaller ball represents the moon, and the larger ball represents Earth. Hold the larger clay ball on your hand and rotate the straw until the larger ball lifts off your hand. Rotate the model so that the earth and moon are both in motion.

- What do you think would happen to the smaller ball if it flew off the model?
- What do you think would happen to the larger ball if the smaller one flew off?
- How would you make a model of the sun and Earth or another planet such as Mars?

Centripetal Spinners *(cont.)*

Ultra Spinners

Make a model spinner using one large paper clip on top, two feet (61 cm) of fishline, and 12 large paper clips on the bottom. Make a reinforced straw as you did before or use a three-inch (8 cm) piece of tubing for a stronger rotating object.

Spin your model and keep adding large paper clips.

Can you spin as many as 20 large paper clips with only one large one on the top?

Note: Do this activity outside.

Make a model with three large paper clips on top and a cup below as shown in this illustration.

- Fill the cup ¹/₃ full of water.
- Try rotating the model.
- Fill the cup ¹/₂ full and rotate the model.
- Can you fill the cup almost full and still make the model work?

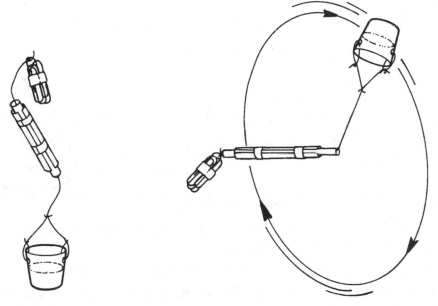

- Hold the model by the top. Make sure the cup of water is half full and hanging evenly.
- Try spinning the cup vertically around so that it is upside down as shown in the illustration. Can you do this without spilling the water?
- Can you spin the cup vertically with a full cup of water without spilling the water?

Centripetal Spin-Off

Create your own model spinner. Be imaginative. Try a variety of different or unusual materials.

- Try heavy objects such as balls, washers, or books.
- Try other flexible tubes.
- Have a spin-off with your classmates. Compare your models with their creations.

Flying Saucers

Concepts: *principles of flight*

Materials: tagboard or manila folders, paper fasteners, large paper clips, glue, clear tape, scissors, math compass, ruler

Optional: plastic, Styrofoam or paper cup, margarine or cup lids, bottle caps

The Basic Saucer

1. Use a compass to make a circle with a radius of four inches (10 cm) on a piece of tagboard or a manila folder. This will make a circle with a diameter (distance across) of eight inches (20 cm).

2. Cut out the circle. This will be the base of the saucer.

3. Use the compass to make a second circle with a radius of three inches (8 cm). This will create a circle with a diameter six inches (15 cm) across. Cut out this circle.

4. Use the compass to draw four more circles. Make each circle smaller than the one before it. Cut out each circle.

5. Arrange the circles in a concentric pattern as shown in the illustration.

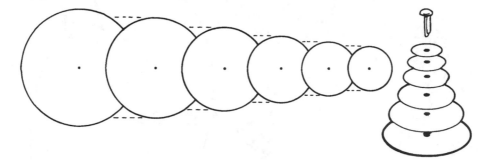

6. Glue each of the circles to the one below it in the stack.

7. Use a pushpin and the point of a compass to make a hole through the center of the stack so that a paper fastener can be pushed through the layers.

8. Fold the blades of the paper fastener down and tape them onto the back of the first circle.

9. Arrange six large paper clips around the edges of the saucer as shown below and tape them securely to the back of the first circle.

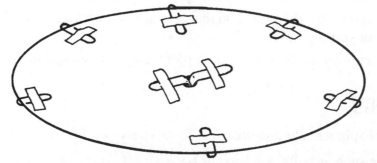

10. Take the flying saucer outdoors and launch it with a swift, Frisbee-like snap of the wrist. Do several trials. Try different ways of throwing your saucer into the air. Observe how your saucer flies.

Flying Saucers *(cont.)*

The Ring Flyer

1. Set the compass for a four-inch (10 cm) radius to draw a circle eight inches (20 cm) in diameter. Cut out the circle.

2. Set the compass for a two-inch (5 cm) radius and draw a smaller circle with a four-inch (10 cm) diameter in the center of the larger circle you just cut out.

3. Cut the smaller circle out from the inside of the tagboard to make a ring as shown in the illustration.

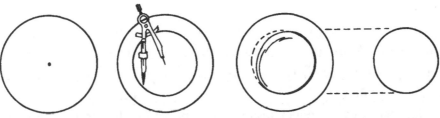

4. Set the compass for a three-inch (8 cm) radius to draw a circle six inches (15 cm) in diameter. Cut out the circle.

5. Set the compass for a two-inch (5 cm) radius and draw a smaller circle with a four-inch (10 cm) diameter in the center of the larger circle you just cut out.

6. Cut out the smaller circle from the inside to make a smaller ring.

7. Glue the smaller ring onto the larger ring as shown in the illustration.

8. Arrange six large paper clips around the inside of the ring. Arrange six large paper clips around the outside of the ring in alternate spaces as shown.

9. Tape down the paper clips to the bottom of the larger ring.

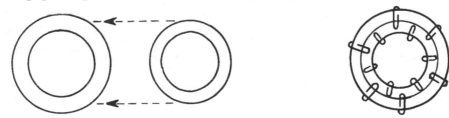

10. Launch the ring with a snap of the wrist like tossing a Frisbee or toss it into the air with a strong overhand throw. Do several trials. Observe how it flies. How does its flight differ from the flying saucer model?

Unbalanced Saucers

Place six small paper clips between the large clips on your flying saucer. Tape them down on the bottom layer of the saucer. Throw this model into the air with a snap of the wrist. Does it fly better with the extra paper clips?

Rearrange the large paper clips and the small ones so that the weight on the saucer is unbalanced. You could have four or five paper clips of each size on one side of the saucer and only one or two clips on the other side.

Launch this model and observe what happens.

Flying Saucers *(cont.)*

Larger Saucers

1. Set your compass gauge at the five-inch (13 cm) mark to create a circle with a radius of five inches. Make a circle on a manila folder or tagboard. The circle will have a diameter across the center of 10 inches (25.4 cm).

2. Use tagboard, manila folders, or construction paper to make nine more circles, each progressively smaller than the one before.

3. Carefully arrange each circle in a concentric pattern with the smallest on top. Glue each circle to the one below it.

4. Use a pushpin to make a hole through the center of the stack and then make the hole large enough with the compass point until you can push a paper fastener through the stack.

5. Arrange six large paper clips evenly around the edges of the saucer. Arrange six small paper clips in between the large clips.

6. Securely tape the blades of the paper fastener and the paper clips to the back of the largest circle.

7. Launch your flying saucer with a snap of the wrist. Compare your results with the basic flying saucer and the ring flyer.

Pyramid Saucer

Copy or cut out the pattern for a square pyramid illustrated below. Make the model pyramid from tagboard or a folder. Fold along the lines of the square to make the pyramid. Tape the edges of the pyramid and securely tape the pyramid onto the center of the flying saucer.

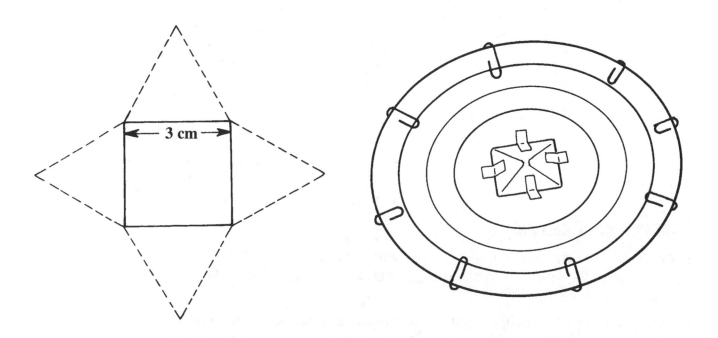

Launch your pyramid saucer. Do several trials. Compare your results with the results of other saucers and ring flyers.

Flying Saucers *(cont.)*

Domed Saucers

Use your best flying saucer or make a new one and mount a dome on the saucer as you did with the square pyramid. Use a plastic, Styrofoam, or paper cup, margarine or cup lids, bottle caps, or create a dome shape from a piece of tagboard or folder. The illustrations show several examples for you to try.

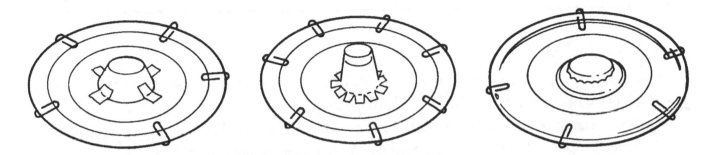

Launch each model. Do several trials. Compare your results. Which domed model works best?

Loaded Saucers

The illustrations here show several unusual models of flying saucers for you to try.

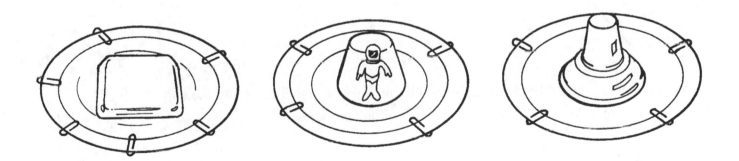

Use your own imagination and your experiences in building flying saucers to create the best saucer you can make.

- Try different materials, such as paper plates, for the base.
- Try putting a load both underneath and above the saucer.
- Try changing the edge of the saucer to create a Frisbee-like curve along the edge.
- Try unbalanced saucers and saucers with shapes that aren't circular.
- Be imaginative!
- Test each model.
- Determine your best model.

Phone Fun

Concepts: *vibrations and sound travel*

Materials: fishline, small paper cups, large paper cups, small plastic cups, large plastic cups, tin cans, pushpins

Optional: large tin cans, 32-ounce drinking cups

Basic Phone Model

- Use a pushpin or compass point to make a hole in the bottom of each of two small paper cups.
- Cut a piece of nylon fishline about 20 feet (6 m) long.
- Feed one end of the fishline through the bottom of the cup and tie one small paper clip to the line.
- Pull the line and paper clip firmly against the inside bottom of the cup.
- Feed the other end of the fishline through the bottom of the second cup, tie another small paper clip to the line, and pull it firmly against the inside bottom of the cup.

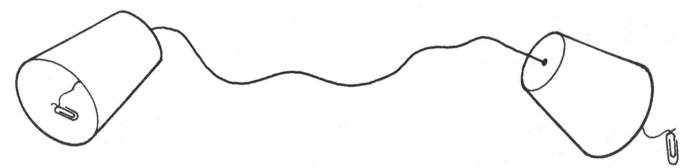

- One partner should hold the cup over one ear while the other talks into the cup.
- The line must be kept tight, or the phone will not work.

How It Works

The speaker's voice vibrates molecules of air inside the cup. These vibrations are picked up by the bottom of the cup, which acts as a diaphragm. The line transfers the vibrations to the bottom of the second cup, which also acts as a diaphragm that vibrates the molecules of air in the second cup. These vibrations are then discerned by the ear of the listener.

Improving the phone always involves trying to make the message clearer and carrying it a longer distance.

Try pinching the line while someone is talking. What happens? What happens if the line touches a chair, a wall, or another person?

Will the phone work if the line gets a tangled knot in it?

Will it work if the line is allowed to get loose? Why do you think the line must be tight?

Phone Fun *(cont.)*

Going for Distance

Cut the fishline off and replace it with a longer piece about 40 feet (12 m) long. Take this longer version outside and try it out. Remember to keep the line tight, not touching anything.

- Try different ways of speaking into the cup.
- Try speaking entirely inside the cup.
- Try shouting into the cup.
- Try speaking in a normal voice near the opening of the cup.
- Try whispering into the cup.
- Tap the cup with your fingers.
- Scratch the cup with a fingernail or coin.
- Which sounds could be heard best by the listener?
- Which sounds were muffled?

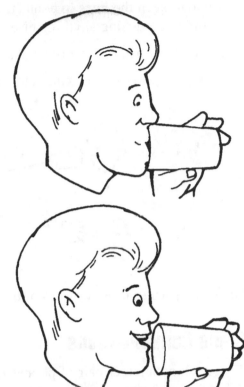

Turning the Volume Up

Replace the small cups or make a new set using large sturdy paper cups like those used for coffee.

- Try out your new set.
- Is it better to shout, talk inside the cup, speak normally, or speak outside the mouth of the cup?

Plastic Cups

Replace the paper cups with a set of plastic cups. Try a small three- or five-ounce pair of plastic cups.

- Test this pair by talking into them, shouting into them, whispering, tapping, and talking normally just outside the mouth of the cup.
- Which sounds are clearest?
- Does this set work as well as either of the paper cups?
- Try a set of Styrofoam cups. Test how they work and the best way to talk into them.

Phone Fun (cont.)

Four-Way Conversation

Take your favorite pair of phones. Find another pair of partners and connect your phone set as shown in the illustration. One line is kept straight. One cup from the second pair is used to wrap around the first line to keep the lines in contact. Each of the four students holds one cup so that the line remains tight and not touching anything else.

Three students listen while one talks.

Try different ways of speaking into the cup so that all listeners can hear clearly.

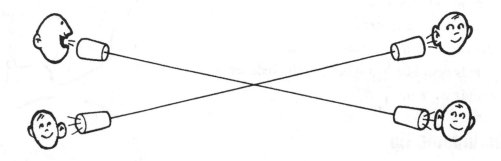

Have one partner face away from the other three phone users and try to identify who is speaking.

Class Conversations

Try attaching another pair of phones to your four-way setup. Loop one of this pair over the line as you did before and have each person keep the line taut.

Five students should listen while one talks.

Try one more pair of phones so that you have an eight-way line. Can you keep the lines tight and carry on a conversation?

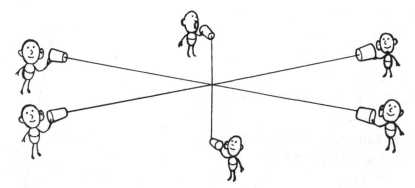

- What problems did you have with six-way and eight-way conversations?
- Whom did you hear the best? Why?
- Can you hook up several more pairs of phones?
- Can you hook up the entire class?
- What happens to the sound as more and more lines are hooked up?

Phone Fun *(cont.)*

The Super Phone

Hook up two 16-ounce (480 mL) plastic cups. Try this pair of phones.

- How do you have to speak with them to hear the best?
- Why do they work better than some smaller cups?

Soup Can Phones

Use two soup cans or other 12-ounce (360 mL) cans to make a phone.

- Test the best way to speak into them.
- Try using a longer piece of line to determine if the message can be heard over a longer distance.

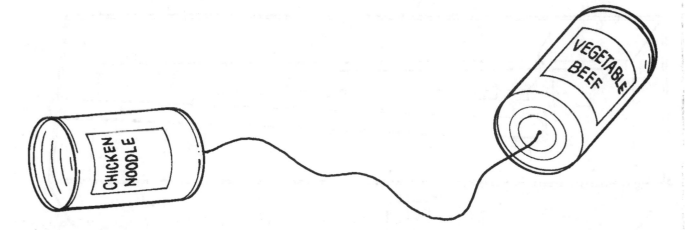

Giant Sized Phones

Design your own set of phones using family-size soup or vegetable cans.

- Test them out and compare their operation to your other phone sets.
- Try a giant drink cup such as the 32- or 48-ounce (1,440 mL) cups purchased at some fast food outlets.
- See if they will work at greater distances than your smaller sets.
- Try speaking into them in different ways to determine which method produces the clearest message.

- Try making an insert for your smaller phones, using a manila folder or index card. See if this makes the message clearer or louder.

Amazing Mazes

Concept: *testing animal intelligence*

Materials: boxes, glue, tape, manila folders, construction paper, toothpicks, flashlight, wrapping paper tube, mirrors, a mouse, small rat, or hamster

Simple Maze

Study the design for a simple rodent maze illustrated below. Notice that it has a designated area for starting and finishing the run.

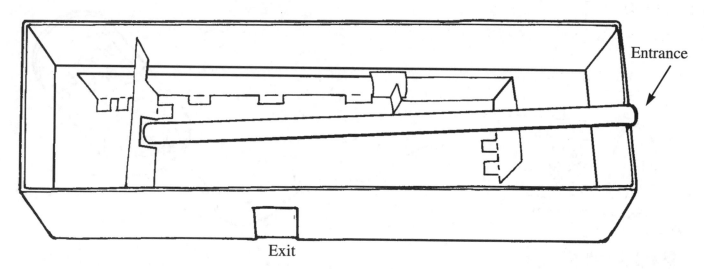

Use a flat box lid or a box about two to four inches (5 cm to 10 cm) high to make the maze design in the illustration.

- Draw the maze pattern as a diagram along the bottom of the box.
- Use pieces of tagboard, manila folder, construction paper, or other stiff papers to make the walls in the maze.
- Cut half-inch (1.3 cm) slits along the bottom of the walls and fold the slit pieces in opposite directions. Glue or tape the walls in place along the diagram.
- Cut a doorway at the places where the maze begins and finishes.

Running the Maze

Safety Note: Never use a wild rodent, such as a mouse or rat, in any classroom maze. Use either a classroom rodent, a gentle pet belonging to a classmate, or an animal purchased from a pet store.

- Use a pet mouse, hamster, or small pet rat to test your maze. Allow the rodent to become familiar with the smell and touch of your hands. Do not just grab it. Gently pick it up and keep one hand underneath the animal.
- Carefully place the rodent at the start of your maze. Do not push, goad, poke, or yell at the animal. It will only become scared and confused.

Amazing Mazes *(cont.)*

Timing the Run

- After the animal has become familiar with the maze, you can time the run by writing down the starting time and the finishing time to the second.
- Allow the animal to try the maze two or three times in a row. Time each run and compare results. Does the animal get quicker with each trial?
- Do not allow the animal to get tired from running the maze many times. Try running a second animal through the maze. Allow it to get familiar with the maze and then time it for several trials. Run a third animal in the maze using the same techniques.
- Which animal seemed to be the smartest? Why?

Z Maze

Study the maze shown here with a Z shape design. Trace this maze pattern along the bottom of a box lid or a box about two to four inches (5 cm to 10 cm) high. Make the walls of the maze as you did the last one. Cut the slits at the bottom of the paper walls and glue them down. Indicate the starting and finishing points.

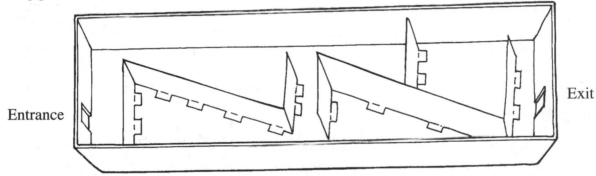

Entrance

Exit

Carefully take the pet mouse (or other pet rodent) out of its cage, put it on the starting line, and allow it to get familiar with the maze as you did with the earlier maze. Do several trials. Time the runs and compare speeds with the first maze. Did this maze seem harder or easier than the first design?

"Salting" the Route

Sometimes an animal will run a maze much faster and with less distraction if you "salt" the maze with a food which the animal favors. You can use birdseed, rodent food, or bread crumbs. Most rodents are particularly fond of popped popcorn. It may also slow them down as they stop to feed.

"Salt" the trail of one maze with popcorn or seeds or some other dry food. Allow the animal to run the maze. Compare results with earlier trials. Did it speed up or slow down the animal's run through the maze?

Amazing Mazes (cont.)

The Three-Looper Maze

The design illustrated here has three loops between the starting and finishing points. Build this design in a box which is wider and longer than your first two mazes. Make sure that the walls are built high enough and connected well enough so that the mouse or small rat can't climb over or slip through spaces which you didn't intend to leave. Feel free to be creative in making your own version of this maze. You may want to increase the number of loops, make the loops larger or smaller, or make them more complicated.

Test your animal several times on this maze. How long did it take him to run the maze at his best time? What confused or distracted the rodent? How did your pet mouse or rat show its intelligence in this maze?

Cul-de-Sac Mazes

A good maze will usually include several dead ends or culs-de-sac which don't go anywhere. These may confuse the animal at first but will usually be avoided once the animal becomes familiar with the maze.

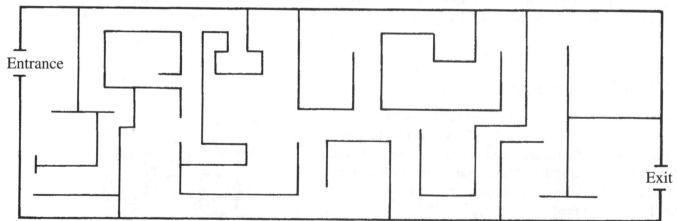

Make a cul-de-sac maze like the one illustrated on this page or create your own version of this maze. You may want to mark the dead ends or culs-de-sac.

Test a mouse or small rat on this maze. Allow the animal to have several trials. Time the trials and compare its speed to the times it made on other mazes. Was this maze harder?

Test other rodents and compare results. Which animal seemed to run the maze best? Did it help to salt the maze?

Amazing Mazes *(cont.)*

Mirrors and More

Add a pair of mirrors to one of your mazes or design a new maze with a couple of mirrors installed. Test your maze with as many different animals as you can. Did the mirror distract any of the animals which ran your maze? What do you think the animal saw?

A Lighted Maze

Aim one or two flashlights at or in one of your mazes or design your own lighted maze. This maze might have a dark-colored cellophane cover to block out room light or a cover that you can lift to see inside as the mouse runs the maze. Test your lighted maze with several different animals, if possible, and give each animal several trials.

Try the maze both lighted and darkened.

The Two-Level Maze

Invent your own two-level maze. You may want to use one of your own mazes for the base and build a separate upper level or start a new maze.

Remember that the ladder connecting the two levels must be firm and easy for the mouse to climb. Toothpicks or craft sticks connected by tape make a good ladder.

Test your maze with a pet mouse or rat. What problems did the rodent encounter with this maze? Was it able to climb the ladder? Did it need help at first?

Gifted Mazes

Create a maze designed for a really talented rodent. You may want to design this one for the most successful of your rodents. Use all of the techniques you have learned in designing mazes. You can build a maze, modify it, or create a completely different design.

Did your top maze runner succeed on this maze? What problems did it encounter? What was the hardest part of the maze?

Designer Mazes

Create your own designer maze using some or all of the ideas you have discovered while making your other mazes. Use your imagination with different types of materials and unusual layouts.

Be creative and imaginative!

Test your mice and rats on this maze. How did they do? What was the most unusual feature in this maze?

Dicey Numbers

Concept: *probability*

Materials: pennies, three dice, manila folder or tagboard, scissors, ruler, cellophane tape

Optional: tetrahedral, dodecahedral, other dice arrangements, other coins

A Flip of the Coin

Probability is the mathematical science of determining the likelihood or chance of something happening.

1. Number a sheet of paper from 1 to 50.

2. Flip a penny 50 times and record on your paper each time whether it lands heads or tails.

3. Count the number of heads and the number of tails. Did you flip more heads or tails? Was the count close?

Number your paper from 51 to 100 and flip the penny 50 more times. Record each head or tail flipped and compute the total number of heads and tails flipped.

The mathematical probability for each flip is that you have one chance in two or a 50% chance of flipping a head or 50 heads out of a hundred flips.

How many heads did you actually flip? How close were you to the 50%?

Generally, you are more likely to come close to the mathematical odds when there is a greater number of opportunities.

Flip the coin 100 more times. Determine how close you come to 50% (100 heads) after 200 total coin flips.

Compare your results with those of your classmates.

Record each classmate's results on a chart.

1. Compute the total flips by all of the students in your class.

2. Compute and graph all of the heads recorded by your class.

3. Compute the combined percentage of heads flipped by dividing the total number of heads flipped by the total number of flips.

4. Compute the percentage of tails flipped.

How close were you to 50%, a probability of one chance in two?

Name	Heads	Tails	Percentage of Heads

    58

Dicey Numbers *(cont.)*

A Roll of the Die

Note: The teacher may wish to distribute a large sheet of construction paper to each child to reduce the noise level.

A cube-shaped die has six faces. The mathematical probability of rolling any specific number (such as a two) is one in six. Compare your results on this page with the odds.

1. Number your paper 1 to 48.
2. Roll the die 48 times and record which number faced up on each roll.
3. Determine how many 1s, 2s, 3s, 4s, 5s, and 6s you rolled.

The odds would indicate eight rolls for each of the numbers. Did you have any numbers rolled exactly eight times? Which numbers were far above or below the odds?

4. Number your paper from 49 to 96.
5. Roll the die 48 more times and record the numbers.
6. Count the total number of times each number appeared in the 96 rolls.
7. Make a chart to illustrate your results.

The mathematical odds suggest 16 rolls for each number. Did any of your numbers get rolled exactly 16 times? Were any numbers rolled close to 16 times? Were any numbers far lower or higher than the odds?

8. Compare your results with those of your classmates. Create a graph to show the results for the entire class.

Two on a Roll

Number your paper 1 to 48. Roll two dice 48 times and record the total of each roll. For example, rolling a six and a two would mean a roll of eight.

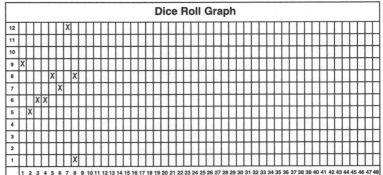

Which number between 2 and 12 was the most often rolled?

Which other numbers were often rolled?

Dicey Numbers *(cont.)*

- Number your paper from 49 to 96. Roll the two dice 48 more times and record each number.
- Make a chart or graph showing the number of rolls for each number between 2 and 12.
- Where are the most often rolled numbers located on the graph? Why do you think it is harder to roll a 12 than a 7, 8, or 9?
- Does your graph or chart show a bulge in the center like a bell?
- Compare your results with those of your classmates.

Three Dice

- Create a tally sheet numbered from 3 to 18.
- Roll three dice and record the total for each roll on the tally sheet.
- Can you discover a pattern in the totals?
- Which numbers seem to be the easiest to roll?

ROLL	SCORE	ROLL	SCORE
1		25	
2		26	
3		27	
4		28	

- Roll the three dice another 48 times and record your results on the tally sheet.
- What pattern could you find?
- Did your classmates have a similar pattern?

Tetrahedral Dice

- Cut out or copy the pattern for a tetrahedral die illustrated on this page.
- Use tagboard or a manila folder to make the die.
- Number the faces on the die from 1 to 4.
- Carefully fold and tape the die with thin strips of cellophane tape as shown.

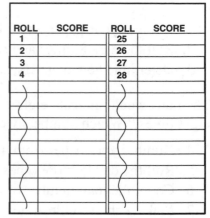

- Roll the die 48 times and record your results on a tally sheet.
- Use the side that lands down for this die.
- The mathematical odds for rolling any of the four numbers would be one in four or 12 rolls per number.
- What were your results?

Dicey Numbers *(cont.)*

Octahedral Dice

- Cut out or copy the pattern for an octahedral die illustrated on this page. Use tagboard or a manila folder to make the die. Number the faces on the die from 1 to 8.

- Carefully fold and tape the die with thin strips of cellophane tape.

- Roll the die 48 times and record your results on a tally sheet. The mathematical odds for rolling any of the eight numbers would be one in eight or six rolls per number.

- What were your results?

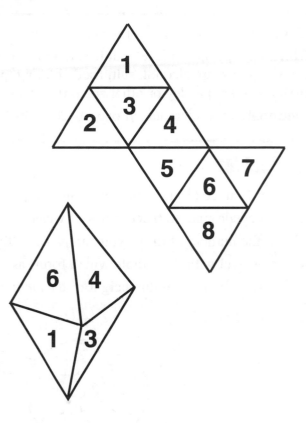

Dodecahedral Dice

- Make the dodecahedral die illustrated on this page as you did the other dice. Number the faces from 1 to 12 and carefully fold and tape the die.

- Roll this die 48 times and record results.

- What is the probability of rolling any one number?

- What results did you get?

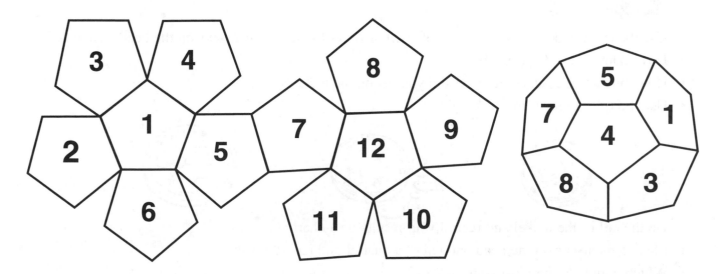

Meniscus Matches

Concept: *surface tension of water*

Materials: pennies, nickels, dimes, quarters, clear cups, water, eyedroppers, meauring cup, ruler, liquid soap, alcohol, salt, food coloring, plastic bowls, plastic plates, small paper clips, tissue, pepper, parsley or other spice flakes, aluminum foil, toothpicks

Optional: straws, graduated one-ounce or 30 mL container, other fluids, other containers

Penny Bubbles

1. Pour one ounce (30 mL) of water into a cup.
2. Use an eyedropper to place drops of water on the head of a dry penny.
3. Count the number of drops you can place on the penny before it spills over the edge.
4. Get eye level with the bubble which forms as you are placing water on the penny.
5. Use a ruler to measure the height of the *meniscus*, the bubble formed on the penny.

Do two more trials on the penny head. Did you get more or fewer drops the second and third times?

About how much of the ounce of water were you able to put on the penny in one trial?

Do three trials on the tail. Make a chart showing your six trials.

Compare your results with those of your classmates.

Coin Comparisons

- Use the eyedropper and one ounce (30 mL) of water to make a meniscus on the head of a nickel.
- How many drops did you use?
- How much of the ounce of water did you get on the nickel?
- Use the ruler to measure the height.

- Do the tail of the nickel and record your results on a chart.
- Make a meniscus on the head and tail of a quarter and record results.
- Which coin held the most water? Why?

Meniscus Matches *(cont.)*

Meniscus on a Cup

The bubble called the *meniscus* forms because water molecules have an especially strong attraction to each other on the surface or skin of water.

An eyedropper holds about one milliliter (mL) or cubic centimeter (cc) of water. The rest of the eyedropper is filled with air.

1. Fill a plastic cup with water exactly even with the top of the cup.
2. Use the eyedropper to overfill the cup and form the meniscus. Count how many eyedroppers of water you can put in the cup before it spills. (The one-ounce cup will hold 30 mL [or 30 cc]. Did you have to use more than 30 mL of water?)

3. Do three trials and record your best results.
4. Measure the height of the meniscus with a ruler.
5. Can you touch the meniscus with a finger without spilling the water?
6. What circumstances affect how much water the meniscus will take?
7. Use a widemouthed, clear plastic cup and make a meniscus on the cup.
8. Can you get more water in the meniscus on the widemouthed cup?
9. Is the meniscus as tall as it was on the regular cup?

Tough Skin

- Sprinkle a few flakes of pepper on the meniscus.
- What happens to the pepper?
- Sprinkle a few flakes of parsley or other spice flakes on the meniscus. What happens to the flakes?
- Tear a small corner (about one-inch square) of one layer of tissue and gently drop it onto the meniscus. What happens?

- What other light materials can you get to stay on the meniscus without spilling the water?

Meniscus Matches *(cont.)*

Floating Metal

- Make a meniscus on a cup. Stop before you think the water will spill.
- Try to place a small paper clip on the meniscus. Determine if it works better wet or dry.
- Try placing the paper clip on the center of the bubble.
- Try placing the clip on the edges near the cup.
- Use another bent clip as a tool for gently setting the clip on the bubble.
- Try floating the clip on a small postage-stamp sized piece of tissue.
- Try floating the clip on a piece of aluminum foil.
- Try floating the clip on two parallel toothpicks.
- Share your results with your classmates.

Punctured Skin

- Use the eyedropper to make a meniscus on one of the cups. Stop before you think it is ready to overflow.
- Use the eyedropper to place a drop or two of alcohol on the bubble. Observe the results.

- Make another meniscus on the cup and stop before you think it is ready to overflow.
- Use the eyedropper to place a few drops of soap on the bubble.
- Observe the results.
- Why do you think the bubbles broke?

Alcohol and soap break the surface tension of water. They lessen the attraction water molecules have for each other on the surface of water.

1. Pour two ounces (60 mL) of soap into a 10-ounce (300 mL) cup of water and stir.
2. Pour the soapy water into a six- or eight-ounce (240 mL) cup until it is exactly even with the top.
3. Use the eyedropper to add soapy water from the larger cup until it spills.
    - Can you still make a meniscus? Is it as large?
    - What would happen if you used two ounces (60 mL) of alcohol instead of soap in the large cup?

Meniscus Matches *(cont.)*

Making the Super Meniscus

- Fill a plastic or plastic-coated bowl with water exactly even with the top of the bowl.
- Use the eyedropper or the small, one-ounce (30 mL) cup to slowly add water to the full bowl.
- Determine how much water you can add before the meniscus spills.
- What difficulties did you encounter?

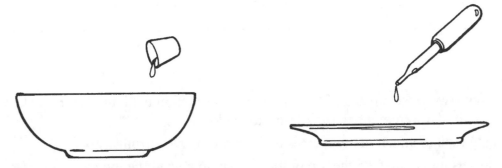

- Fill a plastic or plastic-coated plate with water exactly even with the top of the plate.
- Use the eyedropper or the small, one-ounce (30 mL) cup to slowly add water to the full plate.
- Determine how much water you can add before the meniscus spills.
- What difficulties did you encounter with the plate?

Design Your Own Meniscus

- Collect several containers which can hold water.
- Make your own meniscus on several of these containers.
- Decide which of the containers makes the highest and best meniscus and demonstrate your favorite one to the class.

- Try making the meniscus in your favorite container by adding a few drops of food coloring to the water before you start.
- Try making the meniscus by adding two ounces (50 g) of salt to the water before you start.
- Add two ounces (60 mL) of milk to the water and make the meniscus.
- To make the meniscus, try other safe fluids—alcohol, soap, vinegar, or juices. Try them diluted in water or as they are. Describe your results to the class.

Roller Coasters

> **Concepts:** *motion, momentum, and friction*
>
> **Materials:** marbles, Styrofoam pipe insulation, wrapping paper tubes, cups, scissors, masking tape
>
> *Note:* Styrofoam pipe insulation can be purchased inexpensively at plumbing and building supply outlets. It is usually gray and slit along one side.
>
> **Optional:** other types of plastic and paper tubes

One Loop

1. Slit a six-foot (two-meter) piece of Styrofoam pipe insulation the long way to make two evenly cut runways similar to the one in the illustration below.
2. Use masking tape to attach the two tubes to form a single long runway.
3. Use tape or pushpins to attach the top of the runway to a wall, the top of a bookcase, a doorway, or something securely suspended from the ceiling.
4. Curl part of the runway to form one compete loop and tape the loop in place.
5. Hold a marble in place at the top of the runway and release it.
6. Observe if it stays on the runway until the bottom.
7. Adjust the height, the slant of the runway, or the shape of the loop until the marble rolls freely down the complete length of the runway. Do several trials.

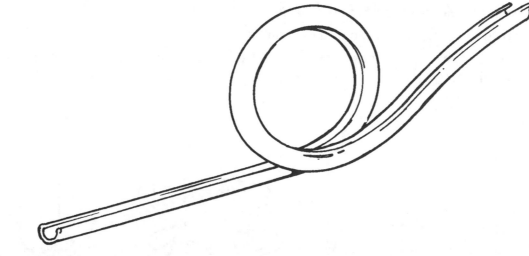

Marble Catcher

Add a marble catcher to the bottom of the runway. Tape a small paper cup or a cutaway part of the cup at the bottom of the insulation runway. Experiment with sizes and shapes until you have an effective and convenient system for retrieving your marble.

You may want to use a sock made of cloth or paper or a longer system which has a cutaway cardboard tube or other device for catching the marble.

Roller Coasters *(cont.)*

More Marbles

- Hold two marbles next to each other at the top of your roller coaster runway. Release them at the same time.
- How do they behave on the runway?
- Does either marble slow more than the other?
- Does one marble stay on the runway and the other jump the track?
- Do several trials.
- Try three marbles at a time and observe how they behave on the runway.

The Two Looper

- Use masking tape to create another loop in your roller coaster. You may have to move or adjust the size of your first loop. Try to arrange your loops so that the marble can build up or maintain momentum from one loop to the next.
- Test your roller coaster by releasing one marble at the top of the runway.

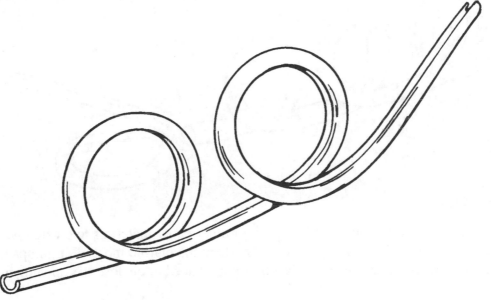

- Keep adjusting the size and location of the two loops until the marble regularly travels the length of the runway without jumping off the track.
- Once you have the marble staying on course, make adjustments in the slant of the runway and the location of the loops in order to increase the speed of the moving marble.
- Illustrate your most effective design.
- Use two marbles with the two looper.
- Can you keep both marbles on track?
- Try using three or more marbles.
- Place one marble at the bottom of the first loop and start a second marble at the top of the runway. Can you get the first marble to push the stationary marble along and down the rest of the runway?

Roller Coasters *(cont.)*

The Rip Roarer

1. Slit another six-foot (2-m) piece of Styrofoam pipe insulation the long way to make two more evenly cut runways.

2. Use masking tape to attach one of the two tubes to the end of your existing runway. Replace the marble catcher at the bottom of the lowest runway.

3. Redesign your roller coaster to include three full loops. You may want to change the elevation or the slant of the runways. Tape the loops in place.

4. Use one marble to test your new design. Try placing the marble at various parts of the runway.

5. Make changes and adjustments to the size and location of the loops until your marble usually makes it safely to the bottom of the runway.

Bumper Guards

1. Use tagboard, paper towel rolls, index cards, or other paper materials to create one or several bumper guards at the places along the coaster where the marble most often jumps the track. You may only need to build up the sidewalls, or you may need to enclose the opening at that point in a tube.

2. Test your coaster using the bumper guards.

3. Place two marbles next to each other at the top of the runway.
   - Can you get them both to stay on the track?
   - Can you get three marbles to stay on track? Try four marbles.
   - Place one stationary marble at the bottom of each loop.

4. Start a marble at the top of the track. Will it provide enough momentum to move any of the other marbles along the track?
   - Will a larger marble started at the top of the runway move the other marbles along the track?

Roller Coasters *(cont.)*

The Super Looper

1. Attach the remaining six-foot (2 m) piece of insulation to one end of your roller coaster.
2. Rearrange your loops so that you can add a fourth loop to the coaster.
3. Tape your loops in place and make sure the marble catcher is attached.
4. Use a marble to test your new design. Do several trials.
5. Make or move bumper guards where they are needed.

- Test your new design several times until the marbles travel the length of the runway without jumping off the track.
- Test your new coaster with two marbles at a time. Try three marbles or more.
- Try releasing each marble one at a time while the others are still on the track.
- Place one stationary marble on the bottom of each loop.
- Will one marble move the other marbles?
- Will a larger marble move the other marbles?

Design Your Own Ultra Coaster

- Design your own ultra coaster by using extra runways or adding tubes from paper towels, wrapping paper, and tubes of your own making.
- See how many loops you can add and still get a marble to travel the entire distance without jumping the track.
- Can you get several marbles to go down the coaster together?
- Will one marble move stationary marbles in the loops?
- Start two marbles at different spots on the coaster. Do they arrive together or apart from each other?
- Compare your ultra coaster with those made by your classmates. Test how well each one works.

Evaporation Derby

> **Concepts:** *processes of evaporation*
> **Materials:** water, Styrofoam trays, food coloring, sand, salt, clear plastic cups, bottles, measuring cup, dirt, liquid soap, powdered soap, baking soda, alcohol, white vinegar, grass sod, clear packing tape, freezer or ice cubes, flat tray or plastic plate

Evaporation Comparisons

Evaporation is the process by which liquid water is converted to water vapor.

Compare the speed of evaporation with this test.

1. Set a clear plastic cup and a flat tray or plastic plate on a level table in the hot sunlight.
2. Carefully measure and pour one ounce (30 mL) of water into the cup.
3. Carefully measure and pour one ounce (30 mL) of water into the plate.
4. Examine both containers every hour throughout the day. At the end of the day, use the measuring cup to determine how much water is left in each container.
5. Compare your results with those of the others in class.

Note: These activities work better on hot, dry, or windy days.

Salty Water

1. Place two clean, flat trays on a table in direct, hot sunlight with your name on each.
2. Pour one ounce (30 mL) of water into one tray.
3. Pour one ounce (30 mL) of water into the second tray.
4. Use the measuring cup to pour 15 cc of salt into this second tray of water. Stir until the salt is completely dissolved in the water.
5. Examine the trays every hour throughout the day until they are both dry.

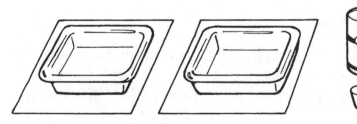 

- Can you feel any residue in the tray with clear water?
- What was left in the tray of salt water?
- Pour all the salt left in the tray back into the measuring cup.
- Did any of the salt appear to evaporate?
- Salt particles are found in the atmosphere. How do you think they get there?
- Compare your results with those of others in the class.

Evaporation Derby *(cont.)*

What Evaporates?

1. Place three clean, flat trays on a table in direct, hot sunlight.

2. Pour one ounce (30 mL) of water into one tray. Add several drops of food coloring. Stir.

3. Pour one ounce of water into the second tray. Use the measuring cup to pour 15 cc of sand into this water. Stir until most of the sand is mixed in the water.

4. Pour one ounce of water into the third tray. Use the measuring cup to pour 15 cc of dirt into this water. Stir until most of the dirt is mixed in the water.

5. Examine the trays every hour throughout the day until they are all dry.

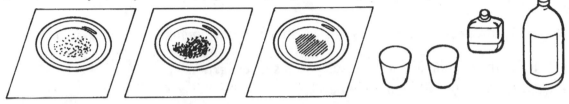

- What residue was left in the tray with food coloring?

- Pour all the sand left in the tray back into the measuring cup. Did any of the sand appear to evaporate?

- Pour all the dirt left in the tray back into the measuring cup. Did any of the dirt appear to evaporate?

- Which tray had the quickest evaporation?

- Why might it take longer for the water to evaporate in the sand or dirt trays?

Chemical Combinations

1. Place three clean, flat trays on a table in direct, hot sunlight.

2. Pour one ounce (30 mL) of water into one tray. Use the measuring cup to pour 15 cc of baking soda into the water. Stir until it is totally dissolved.

3. Pour one ounce of water into the second tray. Use the measuring cup to pour ½ ounce (15 mL) of liquid soap into this water. Stir until the soap is completely diluted in the water.

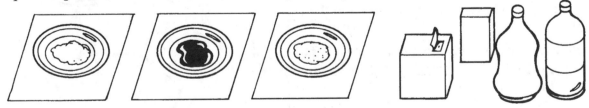

4. Pour one ounce (30 mL) of water into the third tray. Use the measuring cup to pour 15 cc of powdered soap, such as a laundry soap, into this water. Stir until the powdered soap is completely diluted in water.

5. Examine the trays every hour throughout the day until they are all dry.

- What residue was left in each tray? Use the measuring cup to measure any residue you can.

- Which tray had the quickest evaporation?

- Share your results with your class.

Evaporation Derby *(cont.)*

Trial in the Sun

Which of these clear liquids do you think will evaporate first—water, alcohol, or white vinegar?

1. Place three identical clean, empty trays in direct, hot sunlight. Use the measuring cup to pour one ounce (30 mL) of tap water into the first tray, one ounce (30 mL) of alcohol into the second tray, and one ounce (30 mL) of white vinegar into the third tray.

2. Clearly label each tray and note the time they were placed in the direct sunlight.

3. Check the trays every 30 minutes to observe the progress of evaporation.

4. Use a ruler with millimeters marked on it to compare the depth of each liquid when you started and at each observation.

5. Examine the trays every 10 minutes or so as they near the completion of evaporation.

   • What surprises you about the results of this investigation?
   • Compare results with your classmates.

Evaporation in a Bottle

Use three small identical clear plastic bottles for this investigation.

1. Use a measuring cup to pour two ounces (60 mL) of water into one bottle. Place a cap tightly on this bottle.

2. Use the measuring cup to pour two ounces (60 mL) of water into the second bottle. Leave the second bottle uncovered.

3. Use scissors to cut the third bottle half open around the middle of the bottle.

4. Bend the bottle back and place some dirt and grass sod or other growing plants in the bottom of this bottle. The plants or grass must be living.

5. Use clear packing or book tape to seal up the cut bottle.

6. Use the measuring cup to pour two ounces (60 mL) of water into this bottle with soil. Place a cap tightly on this bottle.

   • Observe your bottles once an hour throughout the day. Record your results over three days.
   • Measure the water remaining in each of the two bottles without sod after three days. Compare results with your class.

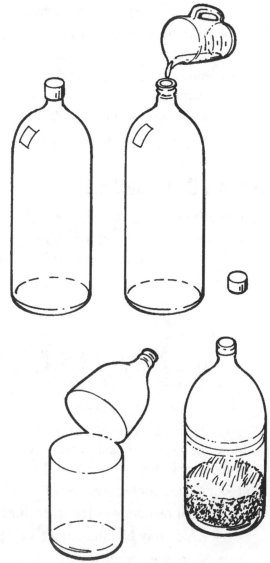

Evaporation Derby *(cont.)*

Icy Evaporation

Test the effects of ice on evaporation.

1. Fill one small measuring cup with one fluid ounce (30 mL) of water.
2. Freeze the cup until the water is a block of ice.

You can use one regular ice cube if a freezer is not available, but you won't know the exact amount of water.

3. Fill a second small measuring cup with exactly the same amount of water.
4. Place the frozen cup (or ice cube) and the liquid cup in the direct sunlight on a hot day.
5. Observe the process every 20 minutes or so until one is evaporated or until the end of the day.
6. Measure and compare the remaining amounts of water. What surprises you about this experiment?

  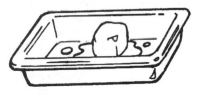

7. Place two ice cubes of the same size in separate trays.
8. Cover one ice cube with 15 cc of salt. Leave the other cube as it is.
9. Observe the ice cubes every 15 minutes. Compare the melting and evaporation rates.

Design Your Own Evaporation Derby

Use all of the experiences you have done on this page and on the preceding pages and your own creative ideas to design an evaporation experiment. You may want to compare evaporation rates for water with different food coloring, for other common liquids, and for combinations of materials such as salt and sand or sand and dirt.

You could also test the effects of wind on evaporation by using a fan or hair dryer on selected liquids.

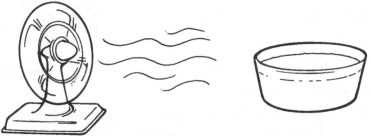

- Carefully record your results and share them with your classmates.
- Be sure to carefully measure results and illustrate your results with drawings, charts, or graphs.

Pendulum Power

Concept: *how pendulums work*

Materials: fishline, large paper clips, tape, hangers, ruler

Optional: doweling or inexpensive bamboo garden stakes, washers

A Simple Pendulum

1. Straighten a hanger so that it is about two feet (61 cm) long. (You can use wood doweling or inexpensive bamboo garden stakes instead of a hanger.)
2. Tape the hanger between two desks of the same height about 18 or more inches (46 cm) apart.
3. Cut a piece of fishline about 16 inches (40 cm) long.
4. Tie one end of the fishline securely to the hanger.
5. Use a ruler to measure one foot (30 cm) down from the hanger.
6. Tape three large paper clips together to form the bob of the pendulum. (You can use two washers instead if you wish.)
7. Tie the bob to this end of the line one foot (30 cm) from the hanger.

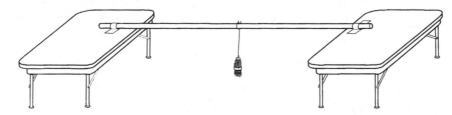

8. Hold the bob the length of the fishline and even with the level of the hanger and desks.
9. Release the bob and time how long it takes the bob to hang motionless again.
10. Hold the bob the length of the fishline again and even with the level of the hangers and desks.
11. Release the bob and count the number of swings the pendulum makes before it hangs motionless again. Count one forward and one backward movement as one complete cycle.

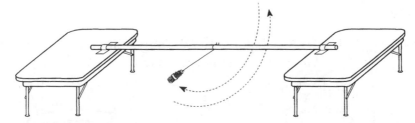

12. Hold the bob above the level of the hanger and release it so that it swings evenly without jerking.
13. Try several angles above the hanger level.
    - How high can you hold it and still get an even—not jerky—swing?
    - Can you hold it directly above the hanger and get a smooth swing?
    - Does the pendulum swing longer if it is released from a higher angle?
    - At what angle do you get the longest period of swinging?

Pendulum Power *(cont.)*

The Weight of the Bob

1. Move the desks as far apart as you can and still securely hold the hanger between them.
2. Move the pendulum you have been using to one side of the space between the desks.
3. Tape six large paper clips together to form a bob twice as heavy as the one you have been using.
4. Cut another piece of fishline about 16 inches (40 cm) long and suspend the bob on this pendulum exactly the same length as the other one. Adjust the fishline until you are certain they are an even length.
5. Adjust the two pendulums on the hanger until they are far enough apart so as not to swing into each other or to swing into the sides of the desks.

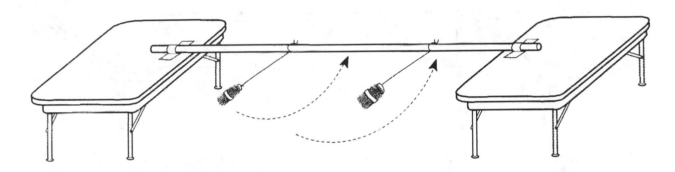

6. Hold the two bobs at their full lengths, even with the level of the hanger and the desks.
7. Release the bobs at the same time.
8. Observe the speeds of the bobs and how they swing.
9. Adjust the bobs if they get tangled and try again.
10. Do at least three trials of the bobs.
    - Do they swing at the same time in rhythm? Why do you think this happens?
    - Do you think the weight of the bob affects the speed of the swing?

Heavyweight Bobs

1. Add three more large paper clips to the bob with six paper clips.
2. Tape them securely. Make sure they are exactly the same length as the three-clip bob.
3. Again, hold the two bobs at their full length even with the level of the hanger and the desks.
4. Release the bobs at the same time.
5. Observe the speed of the bobs and how they swing.
6. Adjust the bobs if they get tangled and try again.
7. Do at least three trials of the heavyweight bobs.
    - Do they swing at the same time in rhythm?
    - Do you think the weight of the bob affects the speed of the swing?
    - Test your opinion by making a bob with 12 large paper clips and comparing swings.

Pendulum Power (cont.)

The Length of the Pendulum

1. Remove the heavier bob. Leave the original pendulum in place.
2. Cut a piece of fishline two feet (61 cm) long.
3. Make a three-paper-clip bob just like the original one. Tie one end of the fishline to the bob.
4. Use a ruler to measure exactly 18 inches (46 cm) from the hanger and tie the other end of the fishline so that this pendulum hangs exactly 18 inches from the hanger.
5. Arrange the two pendulums on the hanger so that they will not swing into each other or the sides of the desk.

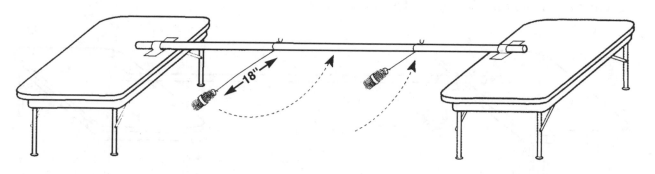

6. Hold the two bobs at their full lengths even with the level of the hanger and the desks.
7. Release the bobs at the same time.
8. Observe the speeds of the bobs and how they swing.
9. Adjust the bobs if they get tangled and try again.
10. Do at least three trials.
    - What is different about these two pendulums?
    - Which pendulum always swings more slowly?
    - Hold each of these bobs at the starting point.
    - You and a partner should each count the number of swings for each bob. Remember that one full swing back and forth counts as one cycle.
    - Which pendulum keeps swinging longer?

Longer Pendulums

1. Move the two pendulums to one side or remove them for the moment.
2. Make one pendulum with a three-paper clip bob that hangs only six inches (15 cm) from the hanger.
3. Make a second pendulum with a three-paper clip bob which hangs just above the floor.
4. Hold the two pendulums level with the hanger and release them at the same time.
5. With a partner, time how long each pendulum swings until it becomes still.
6. With a partner, count the number of complete swings each pendulum makes.
7. Share your results with the class.

Pendulum Power *(cont.)*

Peculiar Pendulums

1. Remove the hanger between the two desks and tape a two-foot (61 cm) piece of fishline stretched tightly between the two desks.

2. Make two 12-inch long (30 cm) pendulums with three paper clip bobs on each.

3. Tie them to the fishline stretched between the two desks so that they are exactly the same length.

4. Tighten and retape the fishline if it starts to sag.

5. Arrange the two pendulums so that they do not swing into each other or into the sides of the desks.

6. Hold the two bobs at their full length, even with the level of the hanger and the desks.

7. Release the bobs at the same time.

8. Observe the speeds of the bobs and how they swing. Adjust the bobs if they get tangled and try again.

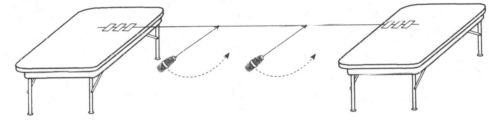

- Do at least three trials of the bobs.
- What happens to first one pendulum and then the other?
- Time how long it takes for both pendulums to become perfectly still.
- On a separate trial, count how many swings each pendulum makes. Do this experiment using one pendulum which is 12 inches (30 cm) long and one which is 18 inches (46 cm).
- Compare results.

Design Your Own Unique Pendulum Experiments

Use the information and ideas you have acquired in this unit to design your own unique pendulum activities.

Some ideas you could start with include the following:

- Make much longer pendulums and test them.
- Use higher structures such as a door frame to test long pendulums.
- Make and test much heavier pendulums.
- Try two-layer bobs with paper clips hooked in the lower wings of the first layer.
- Try finding two pendulums where one moves exactly twice as fast as the other.
- Try three or more pendulums hooked at the same time on the fishline suspended between two desks.
- Try other types, shapes, and kinds of bobs. Be imaginative and creative.
- Share your results with the class.

Illuminating Illusions

Concepts: *retinal retention and spectrum of colors*

Materials: manila folder or tagboard, index cards, markers, colored pencils, or crayons, thin straws, regular straws, tape, paper clips, pencils, pushpins

Optional: small electric motors

Color Wheels

1. Make a primary color wheel using a math compass and ruler. Color the three sections red, blue, and yellow.

2. Use the compass and ruler or the second pattern to make a six-color wheel that includes all the colors of the spectrum or the rainbow. Color the six sections— red, orange, yellow, green, blue, and violet.

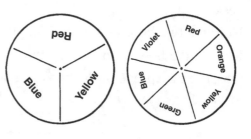

Color in Motion

Try either or both of these methods for putting your color wheels in motion.

1. Insert a pushpin through the center of the color wheel and into a pencil eraser. Spin each color wheel and observe what appears to happen to the colors.

2. Use scissors to make a one-inch (2.54 cm) slit at one end of a small straw. Tape the split end to the back of the color wheel. Place the thin straw with the attached color wheel into a wider straw. Spin the wheel and observe the results.

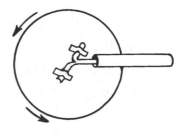

3. Bend three large paper clips at a 45° angle and tape them to a book, a desk, or a manila folder. Tape the part of each paper clip which is sticking up so that loops are formed at the top as shown.

   Use the thin straw with the attached color wheel you made in the last activity. Place the straw in the three loops of the paper clip and spin it rapidly. Observe the results.

4. Mount and tape the color wheel on the shaft of a small electric toy motor. Attach a battery and observe the results.

   - Which method works best? Why?
   - What happened to the colors in each wheel?

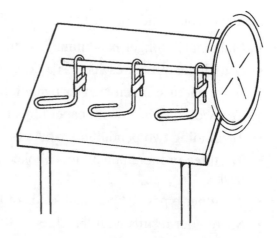

78

Illuminating Illusions *(cont.)*

Retinal Retention

The eye retains an image about a tenth of a second after the image has passed. This persistence of vision explains why the colors appear to blur and converge into a single color. It also explains why the illusions occur during the activities on the following pages. This ability makes it possible to see the separate frames of a movie as a moving image. The same effect applies to animation, making individual pictures appear to be a moving image.

Dots, Lines, and Circles

1. Use a compass to cut out a small circle like the ones illustrated on this page.
2. Use three different colored markers (or colored pencils or crayons) to make three different dotted lines across sections of the circle.
3. Mount the circle on the straw and place it inside the larger straw as you did on page 78 or use any of the other methods for making the circle twirl rapidly.

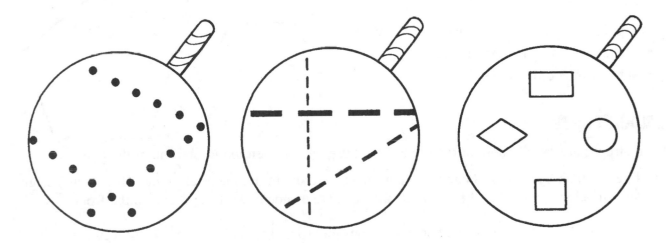

4. Observe the results. Why do you think the dotted lines looked like circles?
5. Make another model with thicker dots, more dotted lines, and dots spaced farther apart. Put this wheel on a straw and twirl it. What results did you get this time?
6. Make a circle and use a dark marker to draw three straight lines across parts of the circle as shown in the illustrations. Mount this wheel on the straw and twirl it inside the larger straw or use another method to make it rotate rapidly.
7. Make another wheel and draw some geometric figures on it, such as a square, a triangle, a circle, and so forth. Mount the wheel on a straw and rotate it rapidly. What did you observe this time?
8. Design your own wheels using colors, lines, dots, and figures. Rotate them rapidly.
9. Share your results with your classmates.

Illuminating Illusions *(cont.)*

Square Wheels and Other Shapes

1. Use a ruler and scissors to cut a rectangle or square from the index card or manila folder.
2. Use markers to make a design using dots, lines, or geometric figures on the rectangle.
3. Mount this on your straw or use another method of rotating the disk. What appears to happen to the shape of the rectangle?
4. Measure and cut a triangle from the card. Use the markers to create a line design on it. Rotate the triangle. What appears to happen to the shape of the triangle?

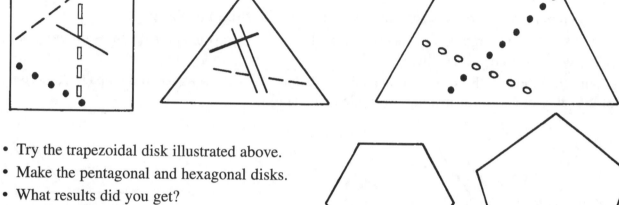

- Try the trapezoidal disk illustrated above.
- Make the pentagonal and hexagonal disks.
- What results did you get?

Thaumatropes

Thaumatropes are rapidly spinning designs which use retinal retention to present an illusion.

1. Use a 3-inch by 5-inch (8 cm by 13 cm) index card or similar material to make the name design shown below. Note that the letters on the back are upside down from those on the front.

2. On one side of the card, use a compass or pushpin to make a hole and push a thin rubber band through the hole. Loop the rubber band inside itself. Insert a second rubber band on the other side of the card.

3. Twist the card and rubber bands until the rubber bands are tight. Pull on each rubber band to make the card rotate rapidly.
   - Can you see the whole name? (You may want to tape the card near the rubber bands to prevent tearing.)
   - Make a thaumatrope using your own name or a friend's name.

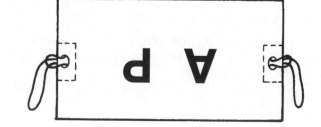

Illuminating Illusions (cont.)

More Thaumatropes

- Use the same method to make the thaumatropes illustrated below. Remember that part of the picture will be on one side and part on the other. The picture with the duck and the egg has the egg on one side and the duck on the other.
- The picture with the geometric figures will have the triangle, square, and pentagon within a circle. You may want to tape the sides with the holes to keep them from tearing away.

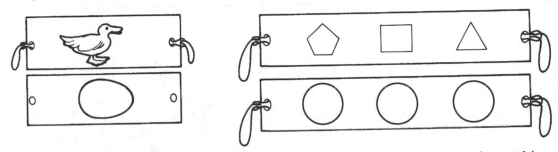

- Make the thaumatrope with the two faces. What happens to the faces when the card is rotated?
- Design your own thaumatropes using other names, large words, and designs of your own.
- Share your best designs with your classmates.

Kaleidoscopic Illusions

1. Bend a small paper clip with one end pointing up.
2. Tape the paper clip to a desk, book, or folder.
3. Use a pushpin to make a hole in the bottom of a film canister or small cup. Put the canister on the end of the paper clip.
4. Tape a 12-inch (30 cm) piece of thread, fishline, string or rubber band to the side of the canister or cup.
5. Wind the string or thread around the canister and tape it in place for a moment.
6. Cut some very small bits of foil, paper, ribbon, or similar material and place them in the bottom of the canister.

7. Pull the thread which will twirl the canister.
   - What does it look like in the bottom of the canister?
   - Try other materials in the kaleidoscope.
   - Make a design on a four-inch by six-inch (10 cm by 15 cm) piece of paper.
   - Curl the piece of paper into the canister.
   - Rotate the canister and observe results.
   - Try other experiments. Be imaginative and creative.

 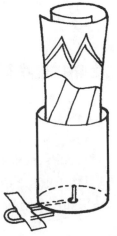

Chutes Away

Concepts: *air resistance and air taking up space*
Materials: fishline, paper, newspaper, small trash bags, large trash bags, construction paper, large paper clips, manila folder or tagboard, plastic bottles, boxes, hole punch or pushpin, masking tape, scissors
Optional: string

The Basic Chute

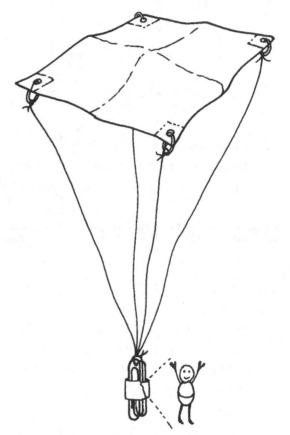

1. Fold a piece of paper (8 ½" by 11" [21.3 cm by 28 cm]) in fourths.

2. Push out the side folded in so that all four folds face up.

3. Cover each corner on both sides with a piece of masking tape.

4. Use a hole punch or pushpin to make a hole at all four corners. Make the hole right through the tape.

5. Cut four pieces of fishline each about 16 inches (40 cm) long.

6. Tie one piece of fishline at each corner.

7. Tape three large paper clips together. Draw a small figure of a parachutist to tape onto the paper clips.

8. Tie all four ends of the fishline together an even distance from the corners. Tie or tape them to the paper clip parachutist.

9. Hold your parachute as high as you can by the chute or canopy and drop it. Note how fast it falls and whether the canopy slows the fall.

10. Stand on a chair or stairs or stage, if one is available, and drop the chute from a higher level.

11. Try folding the entire chute and throwing it high into the air. Does it unfold in time or fall too soon?

Making Modifications

• Try using different paper in your parachute. Try different thicknesses or overlapping two pieces of paper.

• Make a new parachutist. It might be heavier or lighter. You can try using other materials such as pencils, scissors, erasers, a ruler, or a wad of paper.

• Try folding the canopy different ways. You might try to have eight folds rather than four folds.

• Share your best modifications with the class.

82

Chutes Away (cont.)

Heavier Chutes

Use a large piece of construction paper to make a heavier and stronger canopy.

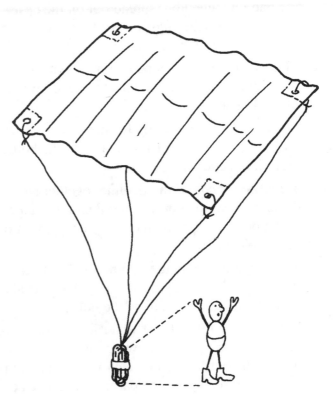

1. Make a two-inch (5 cm) fold along the narrower edge. Keep folding the paper over until you have folded the entire piece. Every fold will face the same way.

2. Fold the paper once in half the long way.

3. Place a piece of tape on both sides of all four corners for reinforcement.

4. Use the hole punch or pushpin to make a hole in each corner right through the taped corners.

5. Cut four pieces of fishline two feet (61 cm) long.

6. Tie one piece of fishline at each corner.

7. Tape six large paper clips together. Draw a small figure of a parachutist to tape onto the paper clips.

8. Tie all four ends of the fishline together an even distance from the corners. Then tie or tape them to the paper-clip parachutist.

Newspaper Canopies

1. Fold a newspaper in half to make a canopy about the size of the construction paper. Fold the narrower side over two inches (5 cm) and continue folding over as you did with the construction paper. Fold the newspaper once in half the long way.

2. Tape all four corners so that the two pieces of newspaper are connected and to reinforce the corners.

3. Use the hole punch or pushpin to make a hole in each corner right through the taped corners. Cut four pieces of fishline two feet (61 cm) long and tie them to each corner as you did before.

4. Attach the six-paper clip parachutist you used before or make a new one.

5. Test your model from several different heights.

Chutes Away *(cont.)*

Plastic Canopies

1. Use a small trash bag to make the canopy. Leave the bag unopened but spread out on the desk. Place a piece of masking tape on both sides of all four corners for reinforcement.

2. Make a hole in each taped corner. Cut four pieces of fishline 18 inches (46 cm) long and tie one piece of fishline at each corner.

3. Use a small plastic bottle for the parachutist. Draw a figure of a parachutist to tape onto the bottle or leave it uncovered.

4. Tie all four ends of the fishline together an even distance from the corners and then tie or tape them to the bottle. Test this model by dropping it off a higher elevation.

5. Try wrapping the chute around the bottle and throwing it high into the air. Do several trials. Did it open and slow the fall of the bottle?

6. Put an ounce (30 mL) of water in the bottle and cap it. Try dropping and throwing the chute again. Did it slow the bottle? How much water can you put into the bottle before the parachute "flames out" and won't open?

Variations on a Chute

- Use another small plastic bag or reuse the one described above and redesign the canopy so that the corners are at the four corners of the open trash bag. Attach the suspension lines and the bottle and test the new model.

- Use a large 30-gallon (113.5 L) trash bag for the canopy. Place a piece of masking tape on both sides of all four corners and make a hole in each taped corner. Cut four pieces of fishline two feet (61 cm) long and tie one piece of fishline at each corner. Use the small plastic bottle for the parachutist. Tie all four ends of the fishline together and tie or tape them to the bottle.

- Test your new parachute by dropping it and by throwing it (wrapped) into the air.

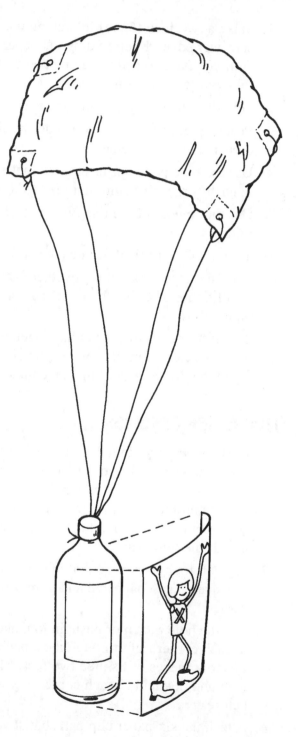

Chutes Away *(cont.)*

Multilayered Canopies

1. Use either newspaper or plastic trash bags to make a double-layered canopy. Make the parachute as you have made others with the newspaper or plastic bag. Use fishline two feet (61 cm) long or longer.

2. Two inches (5 cm) below the first canopy, run the fishline through a hole in each corner of the second canopy and tie or tape it in place. The canopies will be about two inches apart.

3. Test this version and compare results with your earlier models.

Dropping Heavier Objects

1. Pack a small, shoebox-sized box with packing material and an egg (or some other inexpensive but delicate object).

2. Design a parachute to protect the egg box when it is dropped off a one-story roof or a staircase.

3. You may want to modify the design of the parachute made from a large plastic trash bag or to slit open this large bag and use the four corners to make a very large canopy for a parachute.

4. You will need to securely tape or tie the chute to the box and do a few practice trials without the egg to determine how well the parachute will work with the box.

   • Did your parachute protect the egg?

   • What could you do to improve the parachute design?

The Drop Zone

1. Design your own parachute models using the knowledge you have learned making these parachutes. Try different kinds of paper, plastic bags, cloth, and other materials.

2. Try different lengths for the suspension cords and different objects to drop with the parachutes. Consider wind conditions and other environmental factors such as heat, snow, or rain when making the chutes.

3. Test your designs in a class contest at the drop zone.

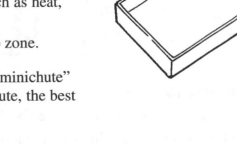

The contest could have categories such as the best "minichute" for smaller parachutes, the best multilayered parachute, the best large parachute, and the most original parachute.

Blast Off!

Concepts: *propulsion and trajectory*

Materials: balloons of several shapes and sizes, index cards, ruler, markers, colored pencils, or crayons, tape, fishline, vinegar, baking soda, tissue paper, corks, small and clear plastic bottles, straws

Optional: manila folder or tagboard

Balloon Rockets

1. Use an index card or tagboard to make a rocket like the one shown in the illustration.
2. Color the rocket pattern and roll it into a cylinder. Tape the cylinder in place.
3. Blow up a balloon and hold it in the inflated condition as a partner gently tapes the rocket model to the top or side of the balloon.
4. Take the balloon rocket to the designated launch area inside or outside the classroom.
5. Set the balloon rocket on the launching pad, lean away from the rocket, and release the balloon.

 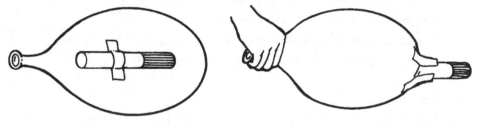

- How well did your rocket work?
- Try launching the rocket again with a different balloon. Try long balloons, twisties, very large spherical balloons, and any other sizes and shapes available.
- Try the slender design shown here. This design curls into a long, slender tube. It can be attached to the top or side of the balloon.
- Which balloon did this model work best with?
- Design your own rocket version. Modify one of the two designs shown on this page or create an entirely new design.
- Try launching your design, using your favorite type of balloon.

- Test it on other balloon sizes.
- Compare your design with those launched by other class members.
- Why do you think that thin, cylindrical models often work best?

Blast Off! *(cont.)*

Guided Rockets

You can often get greater distance by guiding the launch.

1. Cut a 30-foot (9-meter) piece of fishline. Tie one end to the shaft of a pushpin and pin that end in a bulletin board about four feet (122 cm) off the floor or to a tree or pole outdoors.

2. Extend the string across the room or playground to the farthest distance possible. Keep the fishline out of the path of students and tape it against a wall until you are ready to launch.

3. Copy the design shown below onto an index card, manila folder, or similar thick paper. Color it with markers or crayons.

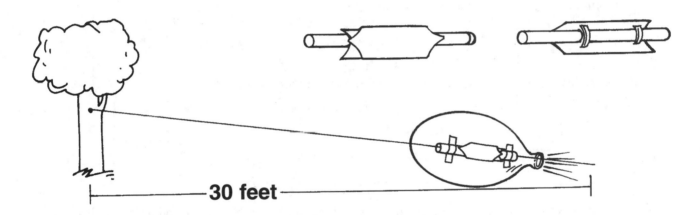

4. Tape the rocket design onto a straw in two places.

5. Thread the end of the fishline through the straw and hold it in place while a partner blows up a balloon and tapes it onto the rocket model.

6. Hold the string and model so that the straw sits easily on the fishline and the fishline is aimed slightly higher than where it is pinned.

7. Release the balloon and observe how well the rocket travels. Did it get to the end of the fishline?

   - Did the straw catch or run freely along the fishline? Did the balloon seem to run out of air before the rocket reached the end of the line?
   - Do several trials of your rocket. Use balloons of different styles and sizes. Hold the fishline at different angles to get the maximum degree of speed.
   - Create a model rocket of your own. Use a different style or type of rocket. Make your rocket longer or shorter, wider or narrower.
   - Try several different versions. Use different balloons and test each of your models.
   - Try mounting your rocket onto a double-length straw that you have hooked together.
   - Try making a cylinder to go around the straw.

Blast Off! *(cont.)*

Chemical Propulsion

Use a small, clean, clear, empty plastic bottle for the rocket. Follow these instructions to make a tube of baking soda that will easily fit into the top of the bottle when you are ready to launch:

1. Lay a facial tissue flat on the desk. Carefully use the measuring cup to pour 25 cc of baking soda in a row down the middle of the tissue. Make sure the baking soda is spread evenly along the row.

2. Carefully fold the tissue into a long, thin tube with no areas where the baking soda is bunched up.

3. Cut four pieces of fishline each about four inches (10 cm) long.

4. Tie one piece of fishline at one end and one at the other end of the tube.

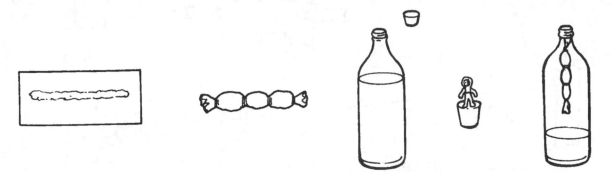

5. Tie the other two pieces along the length of the tube so that the baking soda can't bunch very much at any point along the tube.

6. Carefully fit a cork into the mouth of the empty bottle. Wine corks or craft store corks are both acceptable. Cover the shaft of the cork with two layers of masking tape. This will help prevent any gas from escaping from the pores in the cork and will make it fit tighter in the mouth of the bottle.

7. Make a miniature astronaut from a small piece of straw, aluminum foil, and paper as shown. Tape the astronaut to the top of the cork.

8. Pour six ounces (180 mL) of vinegar into the clear plastic bottle and take all your materials outdoors to the designated launch area.

9. When it is your turn to launch, slip the tube of baking soda into the bottle and immediately fit the cork tightly into the bottle opening.

10. Carefully and firmly hold the bottle pointing away from yourself and others and give it several hard shakes. The carbon dioxide gas should propel the cork and astronaut several yards up into the air.

Blast Off! *(cont.)*

Rocket Launchers

1. Make a small cone of aluminum foil to fit on the cork instead of the astronaut.

2. Measure an area on the playground that can be used for a launch site. Use chalk or a marker to indicate a starting line and distances of five feet (1.5 m), 10 feet (3 m), and so forth up to 75 feet (23 m).

3. Clean your bottle and make a new tube of baking soda as you did before. Pour six fresh ounces (180 mL) of vinegar into the bottle.

4. When it is your turn to launch, stand at the starting line, slip your baking soda tube into the bottle, and fit the cork with the cone tightly into the bottle.

5. Point the bottle down the marked launching area, hold it tightly, and shake it vigorously.

6. When your rocket has been launched, retrieve your cork and cone and note how far it traveled.

   - Did the tube stay in the bottle or fly out?
   - Why do you think some missiles travel farther than others?
   - Try a new version. Try using fewer ounces of vinegar and even less baking soda.
   - Redesign your cone to make it more streamlined or longer or different in some way.
   - Compare your results with your classmates by making a graph of each student's longest launching distance.

Final Blast-Off

Use a larger bottle to design a rocket that you can shake and set on a launching pad before it goes off. (Do not use more than six ounces/ 180 mL of vinegar.) Use different-sized bottles, different types of tubes, tissues of various types, and change other variables to create rockets of your own design.

Remember always to point the rocket away from yourself and others and hold it firmly. Use it only in the designated area and never indoors.

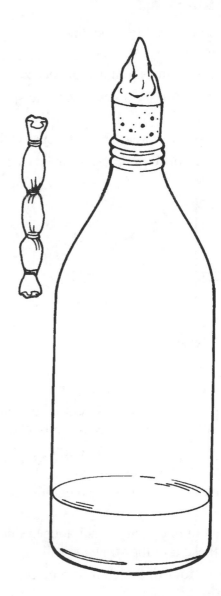

Kites Aflight

Concepts: *air pressure and principles of flight*

Materials: straws, fishline, colored tissue paper, kite string, clear tape, small plastic rings, scissors

The Basic Diamond Kite Frame

The illustration on this page shows the basic shape of the diamond kite. Straws are very light and can be used to make the frame. Make the frame strong by slitting about one-third of the length of a straw with a pair of scissors. Feed this slit end into a second straw and continue to do this so that every straw is reinforced. Put a small band of clear tape at the point where the straws meet each other.

Making the Frame

1. Use four straws to make the middle spine of the kite. Remember to slit each one and tape where they meet.
2. Use three straws to make the horizontal spar of the kite.
3. Make a slit in the spine where the spar crosses it and feed the spar through the slit in the spine to make a T shape.
4. Tape over this area where the spar and spine meet.
5. Use three or four straws to make each of the two shorter sides of the diamond.

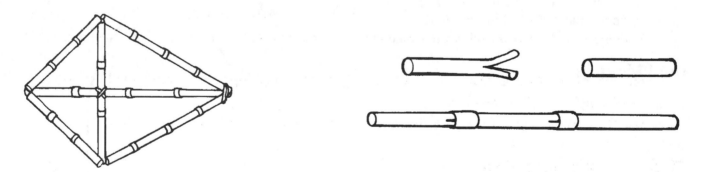

6. Use four straws to make each of the two longer sides of the diamond.
7. Slit about one inch (2.54 cm) at the ends of the shorter sides and feed the slit straw into the top straw of the spine. Tape these in place.
8. Slit about one inch (2.54 cm) of each longer side where the two sides meet the bottom of the spine. Tape these in place.
9. Slit about one inch at each end of the shorter sides and feed the slit straw into the side straw of the spar.
10. Slit about one inch of each longer side where the two sides meet the side straw of the spar and feed these into the straw as well.
11. Tape all four of these ends in place.

         90

Kites Aflight *(cont.)*

Covering the Diamond Kite

1. Use colored tissue paper to cover the kite. Lay the finished frame of the kite on top of the tissue paper.
2. Fold the paper over the frame and use clear tape to tape the paper to the frame and to overlap the paper so that the back is also clearly covered by the paper. Make sure that there are no openings where air can rip into the layers of paper.
3. Use kite string to tie scrap pieces of tissue paper in a bow tail at the bottom of the kite. This serves as a rudder to provide stability.

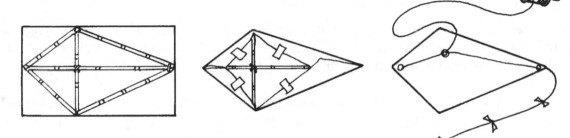

The Bridle

Use fishline to make a two-legged bridle for the kite.

1. Use a pushpin to make a small hole in the tissue paper and tie one piece of fishline to the bottom of the diamond spine.
2. Make another hole in the top of the kite and tie the second piece of fishline to the top of the spine.
3. Position a small plastic ring at the horizontal spar and tie each end of the two fishline pieces to the plastic ring.
4. Tape the plastic ring, if necessary, to keep the fishline from slipping out. Keep the line loose, not pulled tightly against the kite.
5. Tie a kite string to the plastic ring and have the string on a reel for winding up the line.

Flying the Diamond Kite

Wait until there is a fairly strong and steady breeze to fly the kite. Take the kite to an open area away from power lines, trees, and buildings. Face the kite into the wind and gradually let out a little line. Pull the kite with the line until the wind catches and lifts the kite.

Let out the line as the breeze lifts the kite higher into the air. You may need a friend to help you toss the kite into the air if the wind is not steady.

Kites Aflight *(cont.)*

Improving the Model

There are several ways to improve the capabilities of your kite.

1. *The Tail*—You may want to try a longer tail with eight or ten bows connected to the bottom of the kite. This may help with stability. You can also try a different kind of string or fishline for the tail if the kite string gets too tangled with the tail. You might also try a ribbon, streamer, or ladder-like tail instead of the bow tail.

2. *The Body*—Make sure the weight of your kite is evenly balanced. If it seems to always flop over to one side, use a few pieces of tape on the lighter side to equalize the weight. Add a few extra straws if tape doesn't correct the tilt to one side.

3. *The Bridle*—You may want to adjust or modify the bridle if it doesn't seem flexible enough. You can try a more elastic string, such as kite string, a different location for the plastic ring, or a bridle that is also hooked to the two ends of the spar.

If the straws are badly whipped or pulled apart during flight, use clear packing tape which is stronger and less likely to pull apart in flight. This tape can also be used to reattach torn tissue paper.

If the wind is so strong that it is whipping apart the straws, you can reinforce the straws by threading wider straws right over the straws you used. Connect them by slitting them as you did the thinner ones. If you used thin, stirrer straws, regular-sized straws will fit over them. If you used regular straws, jumbo straws will fit over them.

The Delta Kite

Use the same materials to make the delta model that you used on the diamond kite. Slit the straws about one third of the length of the straw and insert them as you did before. Put a small band of clear tape at the point where the straws meet.

Making the Delta Frame

1. Slit, connect, and tape four straws to make the middle spine of the kite.

2. Use five straws to make each of the side frame pieces of this kite and three straws to make the bottom pieces.

3. Slit one inch (2.54 cm) at the ends of the two sides and feed the slit straw into the top straw of the spine. Tape in place.

4. Use the same technique to connect the bottom pieces to each side and to the center spine. Carefully tape all these joints.

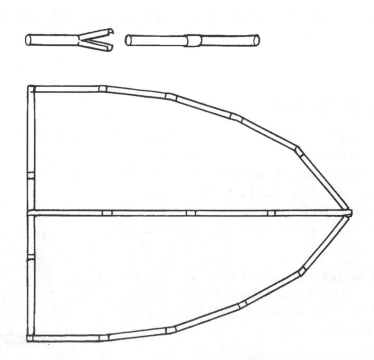

Kites Aflight *(cont.)*

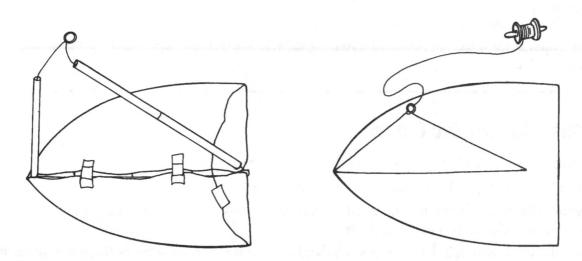

Covering the Delta

Cover the delta design with colored tissue paper as you did the first kite. Lay the finished frame of the kite on top of the tissue paper. Fold the paper over the frame and use clear tape to tape the paper to the frame and to overlap the paper so that the back is also clearly covered by the paper. Make sure that there are no openings where air can rip the paper.

Keel (Bridle)

1. Use fishline and tissue paper to make a keel for the kite. Make a small hole in the tissue paper and tie one piece of fishline to the bottom of the delta spine. Thread two straws over the fishline.
2. Make another hole in the top of the kite and tie the second piece of fishline to the top of the spine. Thread one straw over this line.
3. About one-third of the way down from the top, tie the two pieces of fishline to a small plastic towing ring.
4. Carefully tape a double-layer triangular piece of tissue paper to the spine of the kite and to the fishline/straw bridle. This forms a keel which helps stabilize the kite much as a tail would do.
5. Tie a kite string to the plastic towing ring and have the string on a reel for winding up the line. Tape the ring if necessary to keep the line from slipping out.

Test fly your kite on a good breezy day and compare how it works with the diamond design.

Design Your Own Kite

Use the information you acquired in doing these two models and the suggestions for improving the kite on page 92 to design and build a new kite. You might choose one of the designs you learned or one entirely of your own creation. You might choose to make a larger or smaller version of these designs. Use tissue paper, wrapping paper, or newspaper for the sail. Decide what kind of tail and bridle you will use. Test fly your kite when you are done.

Geometric Kites

Concepts: *air pressure and principles of flight*

Materials: straws, fishline, colored tissue paper, kite string, clear tape, small plastic rings, scissors, glue

Box Kites—Making the Frame

The illustration on this page shows the basic shape of the box kite.

1. Thread fishline through four straws to make the square base of one cubic box.
2. Thread fishline through three more straws and tie it firmly to both sides of the square base so that one side of the cube is now upright.
3. Thread fishline through three more straws and tie it firmly to both sides of the square base so that the other side of the cube is now upright.
4. Thread fishline through one straw and tie it firmly to the upright sides which it connects.
5. Thread fishline through the last straw and tie it firmly to the other upright sides which it connects.
6. You now have one straw cube. Make sure all the fishline knots are tight.
7. Make a second cube in exactly the same way.
8. Use fishline and four separate straws to connect the two cubes so that you now have three connected cubic boxes for the kite.

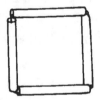 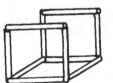 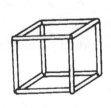 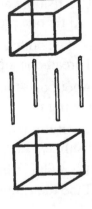

Reinforcing the Boxes

1. Use scissors to slit one straw about one-half the length of the straw and slip it into a second straw to make one long straw.
2. Thread a piece of fishline through one long straw and tie it diagonally through one face or square of the cube.
3. Thread a piece of fishline through the second long straw and tie it so that it crosses the first diagonal straw. It should form an X with the first long straw.
4. Reinforce all 16 faces or squares of the box kite in the same way.

Geometric Kites *(cont.)*

Covering the Box Kite

1. Use tissue paper to cover the first and last cubes of the box kite. Lay the first cube of the finished frame of the kite on top of the tissue paper. Fold the paper over the frame and use clear tape to secure the paper to the frame and to overlap the paper so that four faces of the cube are covered.

2. Make sure that there are no openings where air can rip into the layers of paper. Use the same procedure to cover the four faces of the last cube. Leave the center cube uncovered.

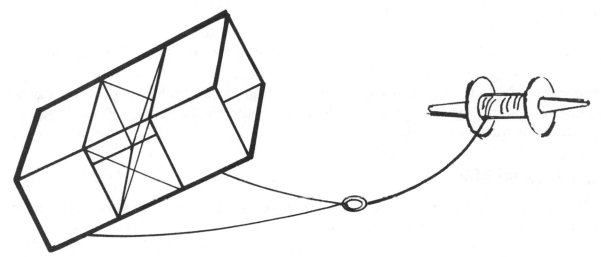

Bridle

Cut two pieces of fishline (one about one foot long [30 cm] and one about 2 feet [61 cm] long) to make a two-legged bridle for the kite.

1. Tie one piece of fishline to the bottom straw of the first cube.
2. Tie the second piece of fishline to the straw frame at the beginning of the last cube.
3. Position a small plastic towing ring near the end of the first cube and tie each piece of fishline to it. Tape the plastic towing ring closed if it could let the line slip out.
4. Let the fishline dangle away from the kite.
5. Tie a kite string to the plastic ring and have the string on a reel to extend the line. A paper towel tube makes a good reel.

Flying the Box Kite

Wait until there is a fairly strong and steady breeze to fly the box kite. Take the kite to an open field or park well away from power lines, trees, and buildings.

Face the box kite into the wind and gradually let out a little line. Pull the kite with the line until the wind catches and lifts the kite. Let out the line as the breeze lifts the kite higher into the air. Let the wind take the kite up. Ask a classmate to help you launch your kite by tossing it into the air if the wind doesn't have enough force at ground level.

Geometric Kites *(cont.)*

Box Kite Variations

Try one or several of these modifications on your box kite.

1. Cover the center cube with tissue paper.

2. Make sure the weight of your kite is evenly balanced. If it seems to always flop over to one side, use a few pieces of tape or a few extra straws on the lighter side to equalize the weight.

3. If the straws are badly bent during flight, use clear packing tape to reinforce them. This tape can also be used to reattach torn tissue paper.

4. If the wind is so strong that it is whipping apart the straws, you can reinforce the straws by slitting wider straws lengthwise and fitting them right over the straws you used. Tape these reinforcing straws in place.

5. You may want to adjust or modify the bridle if it doesn't seem flexible enough. You can try a more elastic string, such as kite string, a different location for the plastic ring, or a bridle that is attached in a different location.

The Tetrahedral Kite

The tetrahedral kite is made from three cells each of which is a tetrahedron. Each of these triangular prisms is quite strong and very good at catching the wind.

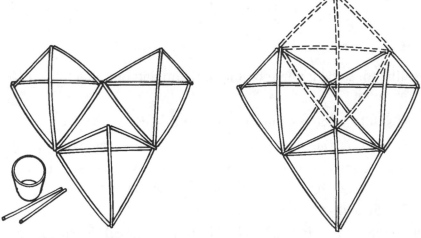

Making the Tetrahedral Cell

1. Thread fishline through three straws and tie them to make the triangular base of the cell.

2. Thread fishline through two more straws and tie it firmly to two sides of the triangular base so that one side of the cell is now upright.

3. Thread fishline through one more straw and tie it firmly to the upright side and the base so that a triangular prism or tetrahedron is now formed. Make sure all the fishline knots are tight.

4. Make three more tetrahedral cells in exactly the same way.

5. Arrange three cells on the bottom and one cell on top as shown in the illustration.

6. Use pieces of fishline to firmly connect each of the bottom cells and to connect the top cell to each of the bottom cells.

Geometric Kites (cont.)

Covering the Tetrahedral Kite

Use tissue paper to cover two upright faces of the tetrahedron. Fold the paper over the two faces and use clear tape to tape the paper to the frame and to overlap the paper so that the faces are clearly covered. Use the same procedure to cover the two faces of each tetrahedron. All covered faces must be in the same direction.

Bridle

Cut two pieces of fishline about one foot (30 cm) long to make a two-legged bridle for the kite. Tie one piece of fishline to the top corner of the top cell. Tie one piece of fishline to the bottom corner of the outside bottom cell. Place a small plastic towing ring near the outside bottom of the top cell and tie each piece of fishline loosely to it. Let the fishline dangle away from the paper-covered spine of the kite. Tie a kite string to the plastic ring and have the string on a reel for letting out the line. Tape the plastic ring if it lets the string slip out of the ring.

Flying the Tetrahedral Kite

Wait until there is a fairly strong and steady breeze to fly this kind of kite. Take the kite to an open area away from power lines, trees, and buildings. Face the kite into the wind and gradually let out a little line. Pull the kite with the line until the wind catches and lifts the kite. Let out the line as the breeze lifts the kite higher into the air. Ask a classmate to help you launch a kite by tossing it into the air if the wind doesn't have enough force at ground level.

A Bigger and Better Tetrahedral Kite

When Alexander Graham Bell invented this kite, he made one that was big enough to carry a man. You can make a bigger and better version by adding cells to your existing kite. Add one layer of six more cells to make a three-layer kite. Add another layer of 10 more cells to make a four-layer kite.

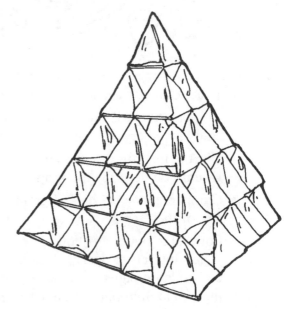

You can try different bridle arrangements and different methods of getting it airborne.

Crystal Gardens

Concept: *properties of crystals*

Materials: bluing, ammonia, water, cups, salt, rock salt, Epsom salts, straws, magnifying glass, sugar, measuring cup, black construction paper, paper plate, string, paper towels, green ammonia, tape, cotton swabs, Styrofoam tray, food coloring, facial tissues

Optional: craft sticks, aquarium salt, ammoniated window cleaner, microscope, flat trays, other common household crystals

Simple Crystals

Salt is a common crystal with a cubic shape.

Use the magnifying glass to examine a few crystals of salt. Feel them with your fingers.

1. Use the measuring cup to pour three ounces (90 mL) of water into a small cup.
2. Use the measuring cup to pour 30 cc of salt into the water. Use a craft stick or straw to stir the salty water until all or nearly all of the salt has been dissolved.
3. Lay a piece of black construction paper on a paper or plastic plate.
4. Pour the salty liquid slowly onto the paper in the plate. Do not pour out undissolved salt.
5. Leave the plate in a warm place for several days for evaporation to occur.

6. Examine the paper as the liquid starts to evaporate and later when it is totally dry. What does it look like? Can you see any stacks of salt crystals?

   - Compare these crystals with the salt crystals you started with. Use the magnifying glass to study some crystals of rock salt. How are they alike? How are they different?
   - Use the magnifying glass to compare the salt and rock salt crystals with Epsom salts. How would you describe the shape of Epsom salts?
   - Compare some crystals of granulated sugar with the various salt crystals. Can you identify any of these crystals by feel? Which ones can you identify?
   - Pour three ounces (90 mL) of water into a small cup and stir 30 cc of Epsom salts into the water until all or nearly all of the Epsom salts has been dissolved. Lay a piece of black construction paper on a paper plate and pour the salty liquid slowly onto the paper in the plate. Do not pour out undissolved Epsom salts. Leave the plate in a warm place for evaporation to occur. What shape is formed by the dried Epsom salts?

Crystal Gardens *(cont.)*

Crystals on a String

1. Use a measuring cup to pour three ounces (90 mL) of warm or hot water into a clear plastic cup or in a flat Styrofoam tray.

2. Stir in a few drops of food coloring.

3. Use the measuring cup to pour in 30 cc of sugar crystals. Stir the solution until all the sugar is dissolved in the colored water.

4. Tape a straw across the top of the plastic tray.

5. Tie string on the straw and dangle it into the water. It should touch the bottom of the cup.

6. Tear a small piece of white paper towel and twist it into a "string" of toweling as shown in the illustration.

7. Tie the toweling to the straw and dangle it into the solution so that it touches the bottom of the cup.

8. Tape a cotton swab to the straw and put the other end in the solution.

9. Place the cup in a warm area so that evaporation can occur.

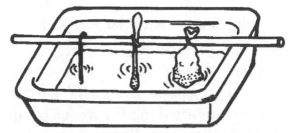

- Examine the string and paper towel as the solution starts to evaporate. Did any crystals form on either material? How many days did it take for the crystals to be visible? What do the crystals look like?

- Try the same experiment with other crystals such as those used for fruit drinks, salt, rock salt, Epsom salts, and other crystals you can find. Remember to use three ounces (90 mL) of hot water and 30 cc of the crystal you are using. Make each solution in a separate tray or cup.

- Which of the other materials yielded some kind of crystal formation?

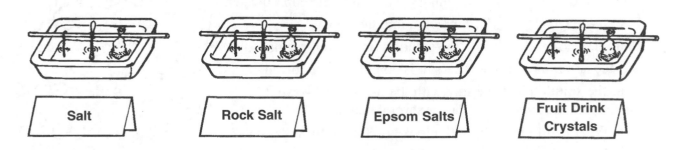

Salt   Rock Salt   Epsom Salts   Fruit Drink Crystals

Crystal Gardens *(cont.)*

Simple Gardens

1. Place several balled-up facial tissues in a flat Styrofoam tray or bowl and set aside.
2. Use a measuring cup to pour one ounce (30 mL) of water into a clear plastic cup.
   - Add one ounce (30 mL) of laundry bluing into the cup of water.
   - Add ½ ounce (15 mL) of ammonia into the cup.
   - Add 30 cc of salt into the solution.

Stir the solution until the salt is completely dissolved. Pour the solution into the tray with the tissues and leave it outside in hot, direct sunlight for several hours.

Examine the tray when the fluid is dry. Puffy white crystals should be evident.

- Did any crystals grow on the outside of the tray? Break a few of the crystals off and examine them with your magnifying glass (or microscope if you have one).
- How do they feel? Can you see a shape? Do you think more crystals will grow?
- A few days after your crystal garden seems to have stopped growing, you may sometimes stimulate more growth by spraying a thin film of water on it or by adding a little ammonia.

Rock Gardens

Try making this crystal garden with rock salt.

1. Place several balled up facial tissues in another flat Styrofoam tray.
2. Pour one ounce (30 mL) of water into a clear plastic cup.
3. Pour one ounce (30 mL) of laundry bluing into the cup of water.
4. Pour ½ ounce (15 mL) of ammonia into the cup.
5. Pour 30 cc of rock salt into the solution (instead of regular salt).
6. Stir the solution until the rock salt is completely dissolved.
7. Pour the solution into the tray with the tissues and leave it outside in hot, direct sunlight for several hours.
   - What is different about the look and feel of these crystals?
   - Do you have as many crystals?

Crystal Gardens *(cont.)*

Garden Varieties

Try making other crystal gardens with the ingredients which follow below. (Always stir the solution until all salt is completely dissolved and always pour the solution into the tray with the tissues and leave it outside in hot, direct sunlight for several hours.)

Dashes of Color

1. Pour one ounce (30 mL) of water into a clear plastic cup.
2. Pour one ounce (30 mL of laundry bluing into the cup of water.
3. Pour ½ ounce (15 mL) of ammonia into the cup.
4. Stir 30 cc of salt into the solution.
5. Add several drops of food coloring—either one or several colors—to the solution or pour it separately onto the tissues.
6. Pour one ounce (30 mL) of water into a clear plastic cup.
7. Pour one ounce (30 mL) of laundry bluing into the cup of water. Pour ½ ounce (15 mL) of green ammonia (usually pine-scented) into the cup. Stir 30 cc of salt into the solution.

You might also make a garden using ammoniated glass cleaner to see if it works.

Try the regular formula, using Epsom salts instead of regular salt.

- Which garden has the most color?
- Which garden has the best crystals?
- Which garden has the most unusual crystals?

Designing Your Own Formula

Design your own formula for a crystal garden. Change the amounts, the types of material used, and even the material in the tray. Be sure to keep a record of exactly how much you use of each ingredient.

- Try growing the gardens on pieces of charcoal, pieces of brick, or other types of paper.
- Try using twice as much ammonia in the formula or half as much.
- Try using aquarium salt or ocean salt instead of the regular salt.
- Try using more water or less.
- Vary the amount of bluing used.
- Try using other crystals along with the salts.
- Share your results with the class.

Super Siphons

Concepts: *how siphons work and the physics of water*

Materials: clear plastic tubing, flex straws, tape, clear plastic cups, water, tubs, trays, or buckets

Optional: hose pieces

Note: This unit is very hard to do without a partner. It may be wise to do the activities outdoors to minimize cleanup.

Simple Siphon

1. Cut an 18-inch (46 cm) piece of .5 inch (1.3 cm) diameter clear plastic tubing.
2. Fill two clear plastic cups about half full of water.
3. Dip the entire tubing into a bucket or tray of water. Hold the tubing under the water until all the air bubbles have left the tubing. Put one finger or thumb over each end of the tubing.
4. Turn the tubing over and hold one end in one cup of water.
5. Remove your thumb or finger from that end of the tubing.
6. Hold the other end of the tubing in the other cup of water.
7. Release your finger from that end of the tubing.

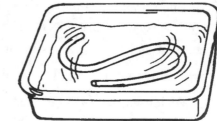

Moving Water Levels

1. Lift one of the cups to a level higher than the other cup and observe what happens. Let the water from that cup empty entirely.
2. Refill the cup half full of water.
3. Hold the tubing in the tray again until all the air bubbles have been replaced by water.
4. Cover the ends of the tubing again and insert each end of the tubing into the water cups as you did before.
5. Remove your fingers from the tubing.
6. Lift the other cup and watch as the water flows back into the original cup. Do not let the cup overflow.

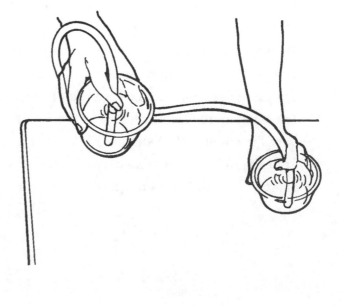

Keep the siphon going by raising one cup until it is almost empty and then lowering it below the other cup.

See how many times you can reverse the water level without emptying the tube and needing to refill it with water.

Super Siphons *(cont.)*

Timing Your Siphons

1. Use two larger 12-ounce or 16-ounce (360 mL or 480 mL) cups and your tubing.
2. Fill each cup half full of water as before and fill the tube with water. Place the tube in each cup as you did before.
3. Hold one cup three inches (8 cm) higher and time the rate of flow until the lower cup is filled.
4. Refill your tubing. Put it again into the half-full cups.
5. Hold one cup much higher than the other and time how long it takes to empty.
6. What sound occurs when one cup is empty? What do you think causes that sound?
7. Fill each of the larger cups about ¾ full of water.
8. Fill the siphon with water and insert the ends into the cups. Keep the cups moving up and down.
   - How long can you keep the siphon running before the tube gets empty?
   - Investigate the smallest amount of water you can leave in a cup and still keep the siphon running.

Moving More Water

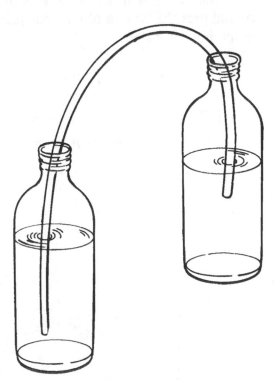

1. Fill two clear plastic quart or liter bottles ¾ full of water. Fill the siphon with water and insert it into the bottles. You will probably have to try this several times before you can get it to work. You have to be quick or the siphon will empty before the tubing gets under water.
2. Keep both ends of the tubing covered and hold it vertically. Place the lower end in one bottle as you release your thumb on that end. Keep the other end covered and lower it to the other bottle below the level of the first bottle. Put the tubing in this bottle and test that the siphon is working. Keep moving the bottles up and down.
   - Can you keep the siphon working three minutes or more without running the tube out of water?
   - Investigate how little water you can leave in a bottle and still keep the siphon running.

Super Siphons *(cont.)*

Siphon Jobs

1. Find a small aquarium, a bucket, pail, or tray. Fill it with water until it is nearly full.

2. Fill your siphon tubing with water and put one end in the container full of water. Use the other end to fill a cup, a bottle, and other containers with water.

   - Why do you have to lift the bucket as it gets low on water?

   - Would it work better if it were sitting on a chair or some other raised object?

3. Fill your large bucket or tub again and take it outside. Fill the tubing with water again and use your siphon to water a tree or some plants.

   - Can you use the siphon to wash off a section of sidewalk?

   - In what directions can you hold the tubing and keep it full or almost full?

   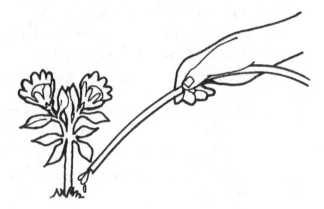

4. Place some sand or fine dirt in the bottom of your large container of water. Fill the container and let some of the sand or dirt settle to the bottom.

5. Fill your tubing with water, set one end of the tubing near the bottom of the container, and start emptying the water.

   - Does the siphon pick up any of the sand or dirt?

   - Fill the container again. Can you get the siphon to clean out all or most of the sand and dirt?

   - How would you use a siphon to empty an aquarium?

   - Are there any chores at home that you could use a siphon to help you with?

Super Siphons *(cont.)*

Straw Siphons

A straw is a perfect siphon. Air is removed from the straw by sucking on it, which allows the liquid to climb the straw. You can also use flex straws to make a very useful siphon.

1. Use scissors to slit about two inches (5 cm) along the end of one flex straw and insert it firmly into the end of another straw.
2. Connect a third and a fourth straw to these two straws in the same way.
3. Make sure the straws are firmly fitted inside each other so that you have a four-straw tube.

4. Fill two clear plastic cups about half full of water.
5. Hold the straw siphon under the water until it fills with water as you did with the tubing.

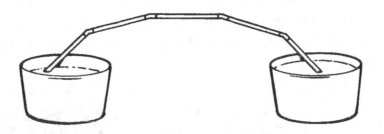

6. Put one finger or thumb over each end of the straw siphon just as you did with the tubing and hold one end in one cup of water.
7. Can you get the water to move back and forth between cups just as you did with the tubing?
8. Add several straws to your tubing and try to create a siphon to empty the large plastic bottles as you did before.
9. Why do you think the water moves more slowly in the straw siphon?
10. Can you hook up two straw-siphons to a large container and use them to fill two separate cups at the same time?

Make a very long straw siphon and use it to do a long-distance siphoning job.

Super Siphons

- Get a longer piece of tubing with a wider mouth, such as a ³/₄- or one-inch (2.54 cm) diameter. You could also use a small section of garden hose. Use this super siphon outdoors to rapidly transfer water from a large container to another container.
- Determine how rapidly you can fill quart or liter bottles with a siphon of this size.
- Try watering a tree or washing a sidewalk with one of these large siphons.
- Find five uses for a siphon of this size.

Testing Towels

Concepts: *osmosis and capillary action*

Materials: four different brands of paper towels, facial tissue, water, clear plastic cups, food coloring

Optional: other paper towel brands

Racing Water

1. Fill a clear plastic cup almost full of water. Place a few drops of food coloring in the water and stir.

2. Carefully tear four paper towels from four different brands of paper towel along the perforated line.

3. Roll each towel into a long, thin tube about equal in length to each other.

4. Mark the name of each towel on one end of the tube.

5. Write down the exact time. Place all four tubes in the cup at the same time.

6. Observe how the water climbs the paper towel tubes.

7. Keep track of which towel the water climbs fastest and which is second, third, and fourth.

8. Keep track of the elapsed time.

9. Do two more trials to confirm your results.

10. Make a chart illustrating the results of your trials.

11. Compare your results with other classmates.

The Squeeze Test

1. Arrange the four paper towel tubes as you did in the first activity. Make sure that only one piece of toweling is used from each brand and that they are about the same size, torn along the perforation as you would do in taking a paper towel for use. Make sure you have marked the brand name for each towel.

2. Wait until all four towels have absorbed water and are dripping onto the table.

3. Carefully remove one towel. Record the brand name.

4. Gently squeeze every drop from the toweling into the empty clear plastic cup.

Testing Towels *(cont.)*

The Squeeze Test *(cont.)*

5. Pour the squeezed water into a measuring cup to determine exactly how many milliliters (or cubic centimeters) of water it holds. (If your measurement cup doesn't indicate milliliters or cubic centimeters, you can use fractions of a fluid ounce on the cup or the millimeters measurement on a ruler to measure the height of the water.)

6. Squeeze the water out of each towel in turn and record the amount of water the paper towel held.

7. Make a chart indicating the amount of water absorbed by each towel.

Paper Towel Siphons

1. Choose any two of your paper towel brands.

2. Position two empty clear plastic cups near the cup of water.

3. Roll one towel from each brand into a long, thin tube. Bend the tubes slightly and put both of them into the cup of colored water. Write down the exact time.

4. As the water climbs up the paper towel, bend each tube so that it is leaning over one of the empty plastic cups.

5. Record the name of the towel leaning over each empty cup.

6. Leave the cups and paper towels undisturbed.

Observe what happens to the water which has climbed up the paper towel.

- Did the paper towels fill each cup as high as the water remaining in the first cup?
- Which paper towel carried water faster than the other?
- Do this activity again but place the full cup of water on a book or some elevated position with the empty cups at a lower level.
- How much water is carried out of the first cup?

Did either of the two empty cups fill more than the other?

- Do the same activity again with the empty cups situated on a book or raised area and the full cup at a lower level.
- Describe what happens to the water.
- Determine which paper towel holds the most water.
- Why might that indicate it is the best paper towel?

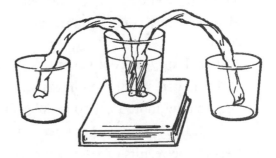

Testing Towels *(cont.)*

The Dry Test

This is one way to test the strength of a dry paper towel.

1. Use four pieces of masking tape to attach the four corners of one dry paper towel to an area between two desks.

2. Allow about two inches (5 cm) of each side of the towel to lie on the desk. The rest of the towel will be between the desks.

3. Keep count as you place pennies on the stretched-out paper towel.

4. Place as many pennies on the dry towel as you can until it breaks or tears apart. Retest if the tape alone gives way.

5. Test each of your four paper towel brands in the same way.

6. Make a chart illustrating how many pennies each of your dry paper towels held.

   • Can you put more than 100 pennies on any towel?

7. Design another way of testing the strength of dry paper towels.

   • How much can you lift using each towel?

   • Do you get the same results using your test?

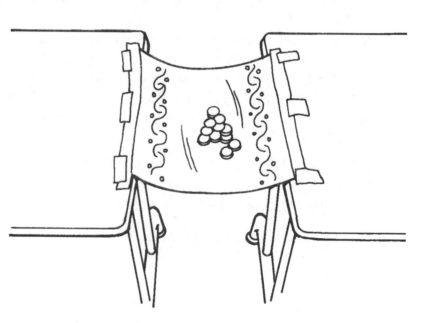

The Wet Test

Test the strength of a wet paper towel.

1. Dip one paper towel in water and gently squeeze out any dripping excess water.

2. Use four pieces of masking tape to attach the four corners of one wet paper towel to an area between two desks as you did before.

3. Place as many pennies on the wet towel as you can until it breaks or tears apart. Keep an accurate count.

4. Test each of your four paper towel brands in the same way.

5. Make a chart illustrating how many pennies each of your wet paper towels held.

6. Did you get more than 50 pennies on any wet towel?

   • Did any of the paper towels do as well or better wet than dry?

7. Record the results of your wet paper towel test on a chart. Compare results with your classmates.

Testing Towels *(cont.)*

Double Layer Towels

Do two layers of towels actually work much better than one layer? Repeat the dry paper towel test that you used on the last page using two layers of each paper towel for the test.

Tape the first layer of towel and then the second layer. Record how many pennies the double layer holds for each brand. Do you get more than 150 pennies on any double towel layer? Which results surprise you? Why?

Test the strength of double layers of wet paper towels in the same way. Tape each layer separately and gradually place pennies on the stretched-out layers.

- Are any of the double layers particularly strong?
- Can you get more than 75 pennies on any wet double layer?
- Do any of the results surprise you?

The Stretch Test

How far will each paper towel stretch before it tears? Test one layer of each brand of dry paper towel in this manner:

1. Fold one paper towel the long way into four layers.
2. Hold one end of the paper towel near the beginning of a ruler and pull gently on the other end until the paper towel tears apart.
3. Record how many centimeters each brand of paper towel stretched beyond its original length before breaking.

Test the stretching capacity of the four brands of paper towels when they are wet.

1. Soak each paper towel. Wring out the dripping, excess water.
2. Lay the wet towel along the length of the ruler and record how far it will stretch before tearing.

Design Your Own Tests

Paper towels are used for many different purposes, not just soaking up clean water.

Design some tests of your own to determine the best brand of towel.

Some of the tests might include the following:

- Strength tests with soapy water
- Ability to absorb cooking oil
- Strength tests in holding different objects
- How many towels it takes to clean up a specific spill

Wind Wheels

Concepts: *moving molecules and air resistance*

Materials: paper, index cards, tagboard or manila folder, ruler, scissors, tape, straight pins, pencil, thin straws, larger straws, clear plastic bottles, water

Optional: food coloring

Simple Pinwheels

1. Use the ruler to measure a piece of paper five inches (13 cm) square.
2. Cut out the five-inch square and draw two diagonal lines across the square.
3. Measure and cut 2½ inches (6.3 cm) from each corner along the diagonal lines.
4. Choose one corner and fold it into the middle and tape it down so that a loop of paper is formed as shown in the illustration.
5. Skip the other cut corner in that quadrant. Fold the first corner in the same way in the next quadrant and tape it down. Follow the same pattern with the remaining two corners.
6. Push a straight pin or pushpin through the center of the wheel and stick the point of the pin into a pencil eraser or a straw.
7. Blow gently on the pinwheel. Blow harder. How fast can you make it whirl?

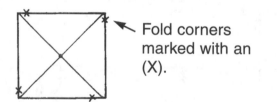
Fold corners marked with an (X).

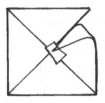

8. Go outside and position the wheel so that the wind catches the loops of the wheel.
9. Run with the wheel to create a moving stream of air hitting the loops.
   - Which system makes the wheel go fastest?

Big Wheels

Make another pinwheel using an eight-inch square. Draw the diagonal lines and cut four inches (10 cm) along each diagonal. Fold the loops over as you did before and tape them. Pin the wheel to a pencil eraser or straw. Test this wheel the same way you did the first one.

- Does it whirl faster or slower?
- Why is it a little harder to get started?
- How does it work best?

Make the largest wheel you can. Use the same method you used with the other wheels.

- Why are larger wheels harder to use?
- When do the larger wheels work well?

Wind Wheels *(cont.)*

Miniwheels

Cut a three-inch (8 cm) square and draw diagonal lines from corner to corner as you did before. Cut 1.5 inches (3.8 cm) from the corner along each diagonal. Fold the loops over as you did before and tape them. Pin the wheel to a pencil eraser or straw. Test this wheel the same way you did the first one.

- Does it whirl faster or slower?
- Why would smaller wheels sometimes be easier to work?
- Do they always catch the wind as well?

Square Wheels

1. Measure and cut out a five-inch (13 cm) square and draw two diagonal lines across the square.

2. Measure and cut 3 inches (8 cm) from each corner along the diagonal lines.

3. Choose one corner and fold it straight down about two inches (5 cm). Lift the fold back up until it is perpendicular to the square as shown in the illustration. Repeat fold in the remaining three quadrants.

4. Push a straight pin or pushpin through the center of the wheel and stick the point of the pin into a pencil eraser or a straw.

5. Test this pinwheel in the wind. Does it work as well?

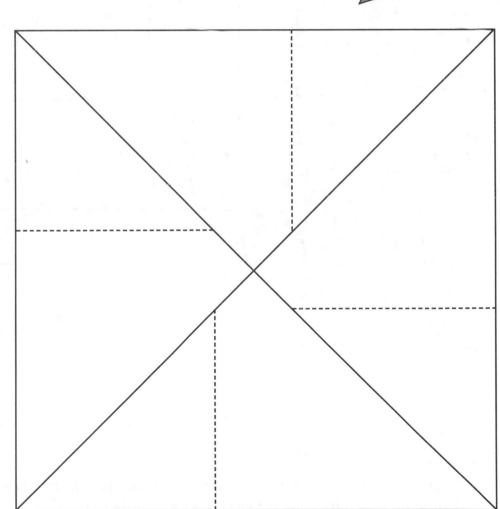

Wind Wheels *(cont.)*

Double Wheels

Use two of the pinwheels you already made to make a double wheel.

1. Slit both ends of a thin straw about one inch (2.54 cm) along each end.
2. Flatten the ends against the outside of one wheel and tape the wheel to the straw.
3. Cut a larger straw about two or three inches (5 cm to 7.5 cm) shorter than the thin straw and thread the wider straw over the thinner straw.
4. Tape the other end of the thin straw to another wheel. Make sure the loops or folds are facing the same way into the wind.

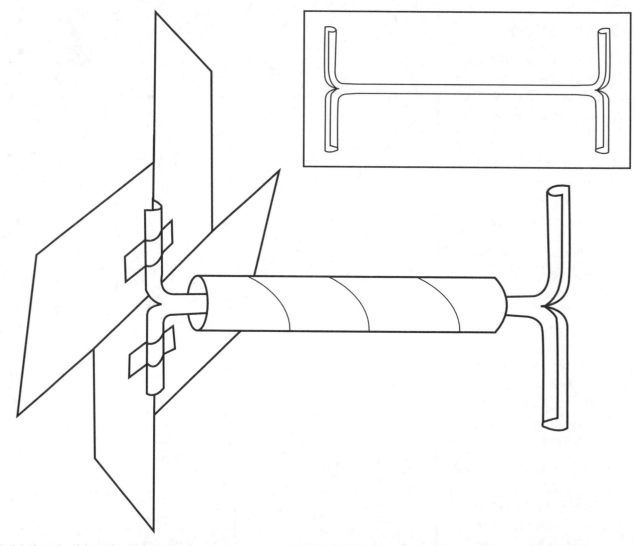

5. Hold the double wheel by the larger center straw and face the pinwheels into the wind.
   - Why is it a little harder to get the double wheel to work?
   - Will the double wheel work when you blow on it?
   - Will it work when you run with it?
   - How would you make a triple or quadruple wheel?

Wind Wheels *(cont.)*

Working Wheels

1. Fill a large plastic bottle half full of water to make it stable. Tighten the cap securely in case the bottle falls and place it outside on a table, if possible.
2. Attach your double pinwheel to the top of the bottle by taping the larger/wider straw to the bottle cap. Make certain that the wheels can swing freely without touching the bottle.
3. Face the bottle into the wind and observe whether the wind will turn the wheels.

If your wheel is not moving very fast in a brisk wind, check these points:

- Make sure each wheel is taped vertically to the straw. The wheels may need more tape or some reinforcement tag or paper clips to straighten them.
- Lengthen the thin, inner straw if necessary. You can cut the thin straw, slit the ends, and thread the ends into another thin straw or half straw.
- You can slit the wider straw, if needed, to get it back over the inner straw. You might need a longer one of these straws as well.

Design Your Own Working Wheels

Make a second double wheel and mount it on a bottle. Use a different design. Choose one of the models illustrated on this page or design your own.

- Add straws to one or both wheels.
- You can add small pompons or flags to each straw.
- Add small paper clips to the wheels made of tagboard or folders.
- Try adding a chain of small clips to each fold or cut of the smaller wheels or wheels made of thicker materials.
- Use a different base for mounting your wheel. You might try a shoebox or giant soda cups.

Card Houses

Concepts: *balance and center of gravity*
Materials: playing cards or index cards, modeling clay, masking tape

Building a Card House

1. Use either six playing cards or 3" by 5" (8 cm by 13 cm) index cards to build a house of cards.
2. Carefully place four cards for the outer walls of the house. This will take several trials before the cards remain in place.
3. Gently place two cards on top to form a roof and to support the walls.
4. Once the house is in place, blow gently on it or shake the desk until the cards fall. Notice how fragile the house is and how easily it is shaken down.

Reinforcing the Walls

Use very small, fingernail-sized pieces of masking tape or clay to reinforce each wall as you rebuild the house. Use only one piece for each wall and place the card wall between or within one small pea-sized lump of clay or tape for each card. Place two or three cards on top of the simple house.

- Try to blow down this house.
- Shake the top of the desk gently and then more forcefully.
- How much force did you have to use to make the house collapse?
- Did it all collapse or just part of it?
- Use some extra cards to try to reinforce the house.
- How can they be placed to brace the card walls?
- Try a triangular shape if you have not used one.

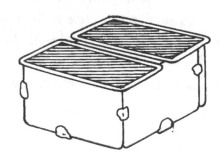

Building Better Houses

Rebuild the house using the tiny bits of clay or tape. Add three more walls to make the house larger. Cover the top of the house with four or five cards.

- Blow on the house to see if it falls easily.
- Shake the house gently and then more vigorously until the house falls.

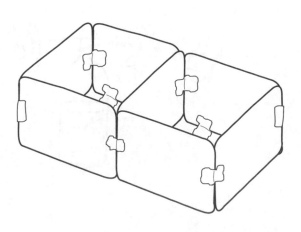

Card Houses *(cont.)*

Three-Sided Structures

Build a three-sided house with the cards leaning against each other and two cards on the roof. Test this house and see if it falls easily.

- How does the shape seem to help this house remain stable?
- Rebuild the triangular house if it collapsed.
- Use two more cards to make another triangular house next to the original house. Use the bits of clay for reinforcement. Place cards on the roof. Test this house by blowing and shaking the desk.

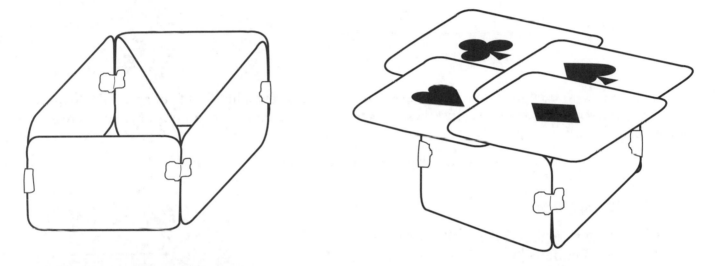

Triangular Condominiums

Use the triangular house shape to build a series of connected card houses. Cover as much of the desk as you can. Use triangular figures that are interconnected but of different shapes and sizes. Cover the houses with cards. Reinforce the cards where needed.

Try not to have several houses leaning on just one card wall.

Test these structures.

- Will they stand under gentle shaking?
- How hard do you have to shake before they collapse?
- How could you reinforce the structure to make it sturdier?

Square Condos

Build a single card house with four walls and a two-card roof.

Reinforce the walls with bits of clay. Notice where the clay is most effective in supporting the wall.

- Does it work better at corners or in the middle of the card wall?

Card Houses *(cont.)*

Interconnected Houses

Build a series of interconnected houses using the four-card model. Carefully connect the houses to use the desk space well.

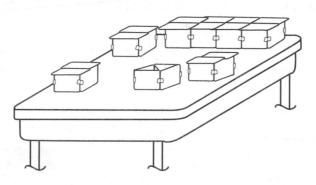

Test the houses as you build them to determine if they are stable and unlikely to collapse. Try to make 12 or more interconnected houses. Test these structures several times to determine how much stress they will take.

- Are these houses as sturdy as the triangular figures?

Two Story Houses

- Rebuild the structures if they collapsed or were damaged. Reinforce the cards where needed. Use triangular shapes to reinforce the outer buildings if that proves effective. Build a second story of card houses on this first layer.
- Start with one house and carefully construct a second layer. You may need to use bits of clay on the card roofs of the first story. Gradually add an extra story to every structure. Reinforce the second stories by leaning cards against other second story houses if necessary.
- Test these structures by shaking the desk. Determine how much stress they can take before collapsing.
- What technique worked best to keep the houses stable?

Tri-level Structures

- Build the most stable four-card house you can. Add several connecting structures on that level. Make sure that all of them are secure, stable, and well reinforced.
- Build a second story on top of these structures. Carefully arrange the cards so that you have maximum stability and well-supported walls.

Card Houses *(cont.)*

Tri-Level Structures *(cont.)*

- Test this layer without collapsing the structure if possible.
- Build a third story on top of the second. This requires concentration and careful attention to the location of the walls. You will probably find that it is best not to place one wall directly above a ground floor wall but rather to offset the cards or locate them across existing walls.
- Test this structure and determine how much stress the walls can take before collapsing.

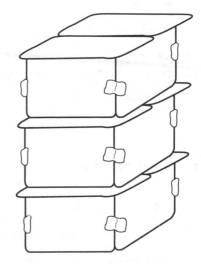

The Great Wall

Use the cards to build a wall around the top of the desk. Experiment with placing the cards so that the walls lean against and reinforce each other. For example, the cards might progress from a square building to a rectangular structure to a square building in such a way that the cards support each other.

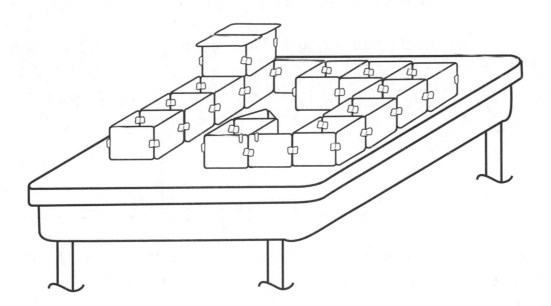

Design Your Own City

- Build your own city on a desk. Create a series of structures on your desk using different shapes, sizes, and designs for your houses. Include some or many two- and three-level structures. Make your structure as stable as possible and as involved and detailed as possible.
- Participate in a contest to determine the best city in the classroom. Share your building techniques with your classmates.

Super Sound-Off

Concept: *how sound is created*

Materials: tagboard or manila folder, index cards, newspaper, newsprint paper, copy paper, construction paper, scissors, ruler, tape

Optional: other papers of various thicknesses

Simple Sound Maker

1. Use the ruler to measure a four-inch (10 cm) square on an index card, manila folder, or piece of tagboard.

2. Use the scissors to cut out the square.

3. Use the ruler to draw a diagonal line across the square and fold along the diagonal. Use the ruler or scissors to sharply crease the fold.

4. Use the ruler to measure a six-inch (15 cm) square on a piece of plain white paper. Cut out the square.

5. Draw one diagonal line across the square, dividing it in two.

6. Cut along the diagonal line. Set one piece aside for later use.

7. Lay the first square inside the two shorter sides of the triangle with the fold of the square between the two sides.

8. Fold up about one centimeter along the two shorter sides of the triangle and tape the folds in place as shown in the illustration.

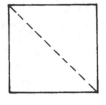 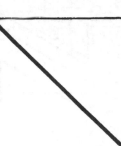 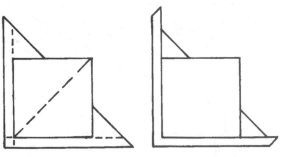

Fold the square again and place your thumb and forefinger along the untaped end of the folded figure.

- Hold the figure above your head and whip the model through the air as fast as you can.
- There should be a loud sound as the inner paper pops out of the folded square.
- Practice holding and snapping the model in different positions.
- Try to make the loudest crack possible.
- Try whipping the model sideways.
- Try holding the model upside down.
- Watch what happens to the paper as the sound is made. A wave of compressed air creates the sound as it is forced out by the inner paper.
- Where do you have to hold your fingers to make the model crack?

Super Sound-Off *(cont.)*

Better Sound Breakers

1. Measure and cut out a five-inch (13 cm) square on an index card, manila folder, or piece of tagboard.

2. Draw a diagonal line across the square and fold along the diagonal. Use the ruler or scissors to sharply crease the fold.

3. Measure and cut out an eight-inch (20 cm) square on a piece of plain white paper.

4. Draw one diagonal line across the square, dividing it in two. Cut along the diagonal line. Set one of the triangular pieces aside for later use.

5. Lay the first square inside the two shorter sides of the triangle with the fold of the square between the two sides.

6. Fold up about one centimeter along the two shorter sides of the triangle and tape the folds in place.

7. Fold the square again and place your thumb and forefinger along the untaped end of the folded figure.

8. Hold the figure above your head and whip the model through the air as fast as you can.

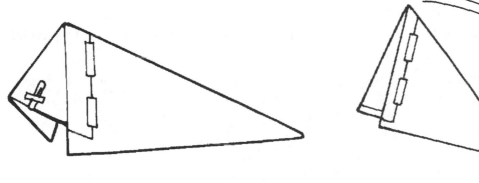
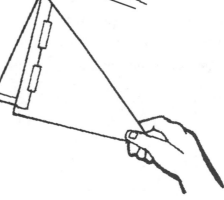

- Is the sound louder than the last one was?
- Whip the model through the air several times to get the loudest crack possible.
- Tape two small paper clips to the inner paper. Try the model several times with the clips.
- Does the crack seem louder?
- Make another model using the same size outer square.
- Make an inner square of eight inches (20 cm) and fold but do not cut along the diagonal line.
- Position the square along the edges as before and tape both thicknesses to the square.
- Fold the square again and make sure the crease is sharp.
- Try this model. Does the double thickness make the sound louder?
- Tape two small paper clips to the inside and try the model again.

Super Sound-Off *(cont.)*

Newsprint Noisemakers

1. Make a four-inch (10 cm) square from a manila folder or index card as you did with the first model.
2. Make a six-inch (15 cm) square from school newsprint paper.
3. Fold along the diagonal and cut off half to use later.
4. Overlap the newsprint over the square card as you did with the first model and tape it in place.
   - Try out this model. Is it louder?
   - Do several trials.
5. Tape two small paper clips to the inside paper and try the model several times. Do the clips make it louder still?

Variations

Make a larger model with a five-inch (13 cm) square card and an eight-inch (20 cm) square piece of newsprint. Cut the newsprint along the diagonal and tape it in place.

- Does the larger model make a louder noise?
- Add paper clips to this model.
- Do the paper clips increase the noise?

Make a double thickness piece of newsprint and tape it in place with this model. Try out this model several times.

- Add paper clips and try it again.

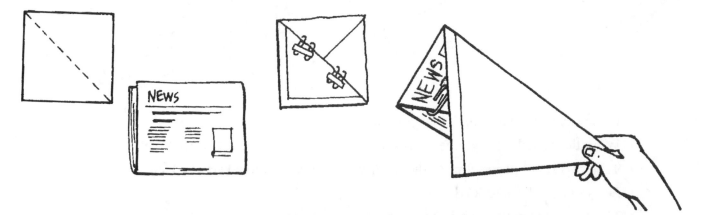

Make a six-inch (15 cm) square card. Crease the fold sharply. Cut a piece of newspaper 10 inches (26 cm) square. Fold it in half and cut away one half. Overlap the two short edges of the triangular piece of newspaper as you did with the other inserts. Tape them in place and carefully fold the model. Make sure your fingers hold the card below the newspaper insert. Try this model several times.

- How does this model work? Try it upside down.
- Try using paper clips on the newspaper insert.
- Use a double layer of newspaper on the insert.
- Which model works best? Why?

Super Sound-Off *(cont.)*

Variations *(cont.)*

- Make another model of your favorite noisemaker. Tape two small paper clips and two large clips. Test this variation several times.
- Make an insert for your favorite model. Cut away the edges extending down from the sides of the card. Test the model again. Does it improve the sound?
- Make another insert for your model and cut away part of the insert after it is in place. Try to cut away pieces that might slow down the movement of the paper. Test this model and compare it to previous ones.
- Make a very large insert for your model. Do not cut away half of the insert. Carefully fold the extra paper back inside the card. Can you get the model to work?
- Make a very large newspaper insert with a square of 12 to 16 inches (30 cm to 40 cm). Cut along the diagonal as you have done with the other models. Fold the insert into the card and then fold the insert again so that your fingers can squeeze the card without squeezing the insert.

You will probably need to try this model several times before you can get it to work.

- Make a noisemaker with newspaper used both as the card and the insert. Use large pieces of paper. Can you make it work?

Sound Off

Use the variations suggested above and your own creative ideas to design the best and loudest sound maker that you can.

- Try different papers such as construction paper or thicker cards or cardboard for the outer holder.
- Try inserts that are made from shiny fingerpainting paper or soft tissue paper.
- Try extra folds along the middle of the insert. Tape extra layers of cards or of pennies to the inserts.
- Choose your two best sound makers for a "sound-off contest" to determine the loudest noisemaker in the class.

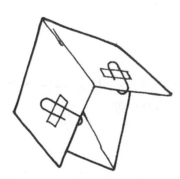

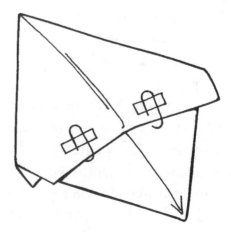

Eye-Popping Emulsions

Concept: *properties of emulsions*

Materials: cooking oil, motor oil, dish soap, alcohol, carbonated drink, measuring cup, clear plastic bottles, food coloring, baking soda, salt, sand, powdered soap

Optional: other oils

A Simple Emulsion

1. Use the measuring cup to pour five ounces (150 mL) of water into a clean, clear plastic bottle.
2. Use the measuring cup to pour one ounce (30 mL) of cooking or vegetable oil into the bottle.
3. Put the cap securely on the bottle and shake vigorously.
   - What happens to the oil and water?
4. Add a few drops of food coloring. Observe the drops as they slowly fall through the oil to the water below. Observe how they spread through the water.
5. Make sure the cap is on tight and shake the bottle vigorously. Observe what happens.
6. Measure and pour two ounces (60 mL) of alcohol into the bottle. Observe what happens.
7. Shake the bottle. Compare your emulsion with those of your classmates.

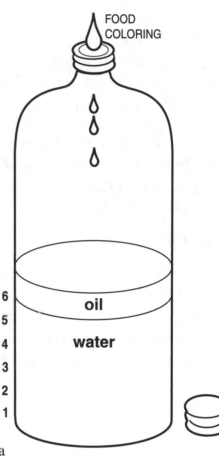

Running Hot and Cold

Set your emulsion bottle in a freezer, a refrigerator, or outdoors on a freezing day for an hour.

- What happens to the emulsion?
- Why is the oil still on top?
- Try to pour the emulsion.
- Does it flow?
- Shake your emulsion bottle very thoroughly and place it back in the coldest place you can find.
- Does it freeze with everything mixed, or does the oil settle back on top?
- What happens when it warms up?
- Shake your emulsion vigorously.
- Place your emulsion bottle in a pan of warm water or set it outside on a warm day in the hottest place you can find. Observe what happens.

122

Eye-Popping Emulsions *(cont.)*

Improving the Mix

1. Use the measuring cup to pour one ounce (30 mL) of motor oil into the mixture. The motor oil is darker than the other oil. Observe what happens. Shake the bottle and watch as it settles out again.

2. Soap is an emulsifier. It helps oil and water mix for a brief time. Add one ounce (30 mL) of dish soap (detergent).

   - Observe what happens as the soap is added to the mixture. Why do you think the soapsuds end up both in the water and above the oil?
   - Where do all the soapsuds end up eventually?

3. Add two ounces (60 mL) of water to the mixture. Add another color of food coloring. Shake the bottle and watch as the material settles out.

4. Use the measuring cup to pour one ounce (30 mL) of any carbonated soda—either a cola or a clear drink. What does the carbonation do to the emulsion?

5. Shake the bottle vigorously. What happens?

Comparing Emulsions

1. Use another clear plastic bottle. Remake your simple emulsion using five ounces (150 mL) of water, one ounce (30 mL) of cooking oil, and a few drops of food coloring.

2. Shake your simple emulsion and watch as the oil and water separate.

3. Shake your first bottle and watch as the fluids gradually settle out. Why do you think the first bottle takes so much longer?

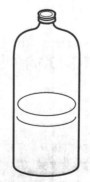

Eye-Popping Emulsions *(cont.)*

Emulsion Times

- Shake each of your emulsion bottles at the same time for about one minute. Leave the bottles undisturbed and time how long it takes each emulsion to settle out. What keeps changing about the emulsion with soap and cola in it?

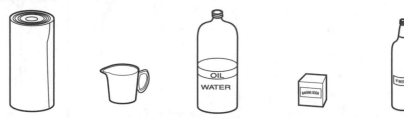

- Into your simple emulsion with only the water and oil, carefully pour 10 cc of baking soda.
- Wipe out the cup and pour one ounce (30 ml) of vinegar into the bottle. Quickly put the cap on the bottle. Observe what happens.
- Shake the bottle vigorously. Watch as the liquids settle.
- Shake both bottles for about one minute. Time how long it takes each emulsion to settle back.
- Time how long it takes soap bubbles or the carbon dioxide bubbles from the vinegar and baking soda to rise to the top and disappear.

Solids in Emulsions

1. Use the measuring cup to pour 15 cc of salt into each emulsion. Watch how the salt settles when it is poured in.

2. Shake each bottle vigorously again for about 30 seconds to mix in the salt. Leave the bottles undisturbed as the materials settle out.

- Did any of the salt settle on the bottoms of the bottles?

3. Pour 15 cc of the finest sand available into each bottle. Shake each bottle vigorously for about one minute.

4. Allow the emulsions to settle. Where did the sand go?

5. Pour 15 cc of powdered soap into the mixture. Shake the mixture for about one minute.
   - Can you tell what happened to the soap?
   - Why does the soap react differently?

Eye-Popping Emulsions *(cont.)*

Examining Your Emulsions

Leave your emulsions overnight or for a long recess to completely settle. List all the observable characteristics of each emulsion.

- Can you find the sand?
- Is either type of soap identifiable in bubbles or the mixture?
- Can any of the salt be seen?
- Where is the oil always located?
- What is sometimes on top of the oil?
- Why do you think the food coloring and water cannot be seen separately?
- What happened to the vinegar and baking soda?
- Shake your bottles vigorously. Wait for the gasses and soap bubbles to calm down a bit.
- Pour ½ ounce (15 cc) of one bottle into a measuring cup and then onto a paper towel or newspaper.
- Examine the color. Does the oil seem to be mixed or separate from the other materials?
- Feel the wet paper. Can you feel the oil? Can you feel the soap? Did any sand or salt get poured out?
- Share your observations with your classmates.

Design Your Own Emulsion

You eat emulsions every day. Peanut butter, butter, margarine, and mayonnaise are some examples. So is the cream in milk.

Place a small amount—about a half teaspoon—of several of these emulsions in a warm area for about an hour. Observe what happens to the oil in each one.

Emulsions are only temporary mixtures. Make your own emulsion using some of the materials used in this unit—water, cooking oil, food coloring, motor oil, soap, soda, vinegar, alcohol, and so forth. Add any other liquids *that your teacher approves*.

Add other solids such as salt, sugar, sand, and rock salt. Try using warm or hot water. Shake your bottle and observe the results. Share your results with the class.

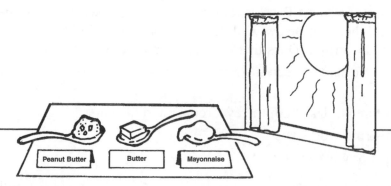

Rivers on a String

Concepts: *surface tension of water and gravity*

Materials: string, twine, yarn, kite string, fishline, thread, eyedroppers, large plastic cups, small paper cups, water, protractor, large tub

Optional: other kinds of string, tubs, or buckets

Note: This activity requires a partner and is best done outdoors to minimize cleanup.

String Streams

1. Cut a piece of string about one foot (30 cm) long.
2. Fill a small paper cup with water.
3. Partner **A** holds the string tight at an angle, as shown in the illustration.
4. Partner **B** then takes the small cup of water and tries to pour the water down the string so that it follows the string rather than falling directly onto the ground.

   • Do several trials until you succeed.
   • Soak the string in the water and try again.
   • Try using an eyedropper to start a small stream of water down the string.
   • Which works better—the cup or the eyedropper?
   • Can you get the entire cup of water to follow the string without splashing off on the floor?

String Types

• Try several varieties of string. Try thicker string such as the twine used to tie heavy packages. Try using it dry and then wet. How well does it work? Try using kite string. Try it wet and dry. Try stretching the kite string. Does that increase or reduce the effectiveness of the string?
• Try using fishline. Be sure to keep it stretched tight. Will an eyedropper work on the fishline? Do several trials.
• Try using sewing thread. Use both the eyedropper and the cup.
• Determine which string works best.
• Which string does not work at all?

Rivers on a String *(cont.)*

Stream Angles

1. Use a protractor to determine the angle at which you hold the string. Start with a 60° angle. Pour the water gently down the string. Repeat several times until you are very proficient at that angle.

2. Try holding the line at a 70° angle. Pour the water. Can you get it to flow?

3. Try pouring the water at an 80° angle. Do several trials until you succeed or decide it can't be done. Try a 90° angle.

   • What happens to the water when you try this vertical position? Does any of the water follow the string?

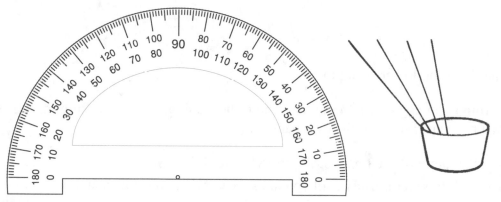

Variations

• Hold the string at a 50° angle and pour the water along that angle.

• Angle the string at 40° and pour the water until it flows along the string.

• Position the string at 30° and pour the water until it follows the string.

• Angle the string at 20° and repeat the process.

• Position the string at the very slight angle of 10° and try to make the stream flow. Do several trials until you succeed or decide it cannot be done.

• Hold the string exactly level at 0°. Pour the water carefully and see if the water will follow the string. Try using an eyedropper for this angle. Why do you think the water keeps falling off?

• Create a chart showing how the water flows along the string from 0° to 90°. Compare your results with other classmates.

Bent Rivers

1. Get a longer piece (about 18 inches or 46 cm) of your favorite string material. Soak it in the water.

2. Bend the string in the middle so that the lower half of the string slants at a 60° angle.

3. Hold the upper end at an 80° angle and try to pour the cup of water down the string from the top. Do several trials.

4. Carefully hold the string at the bend with your fingers without pinching it or use a bent paper clip as a hook.

5. Keep the lower half of the string at the 60° angle and bend the upper half to a 70° angle.

Rivers on a String *(cont.)*

Bent Rivers *(cont.)*

6. Pour the water from the top. Do several trials until you are successful. Keep reducing the angle of the upper string to 50°, 40°, 30°, 20°, 10°, and even try 0°.

7. Change the angle of the lower string to 50°.

Adjust the upper string to an angle of 80° and try to pour the water again. Make sure the stream of water is not pinched by your fingers or the bent paper clip.

- Keep reducing the angle of the upper string from 80° to 0°.
- Pour the water and do several trials until you are successful at all or most angles.
- Try positioning the lower string at a 30° angle and do all of the angles again with the upper string.
- Which angles don't work well at all?
- Which angles are very easy to do?

Yarn Rivers

- Find a piece of yarn about 18 inches (46 cm) long.
- Pour a cup of water down the yarn when it is dry.
- Soak the yarn and pour the water down the wet yarn. Do several trials.
- Place the yarn at an 80° angle and try pouring the water. Do several trials until you are successful.
- Go through all of the angles from 70° through 0° with the yarn.

- Why do you think the yarn works so well? Bend the lower section of the yarn to a 30° angle and go through all of the angles up above again. Does the yarn work better than the string? Why?

Rivers on a String *(cont.)*

Three-Part Streams

1. Cut a piece of string or yarn about three feet (91 cm) long. Soak the string until it is wet.

2. Get a third partner to help you position the string so that it bends around a corner as illustrated here.

3. Start with an angle of about 50° for the lower half and 50° for the upper half of the stream.

4. Slowly pour the water from the top.

5. Adjust the string as necessary to get the water to flow around the corner. Use a paper clip, pencil, or finger to make the corner.

   • Try using corners of different angles.

   • Try a rather gentle bend of 170°. Then gradually increase the sharpness of the bend by using a 160° bend, then 150°, 140°, and so forth down to a right angle bend of 90°.

   • Try a bend which is quite acute at 80° or 70°.

   • Try adjusting the actual angle off the ground of each string as you did before.

   • Make a chart illustrating the angles which just would not keep the water on the string.

Longer Rivers

Design your own river string system using a long piece of your favorite string. You might start with four feet (122 cm) and work up to six feet (183 cm). You will probably need another set of partners. Arrange two or three bends in your river and set the angles of your string off the ground at levels of increasing difficulty.

• Try different types of string.

• Try sharp downward angles and gentle ones.

• Try long, gentle river systems and steep drops.

• Try variations that have the river bending at several different angles and several different levels of incline.

Dirty Water

Concept: *water filtration*

Materials: water, dirt, fine sand, coarse sand, gravel, coffee filters, paper towels, scissors, large clear plastic cup, liquid soap, Styrofoam tray, masking tape, sawdust, charcoal, liquid soap, food coloring, coffee grounds, oil, measuring cup, pushpin

Optional: Styrofoam bowl or other plastic tray, math compass

Note: Never drink or taste the filtered water which will still contain germs and impurities even if it appears clean.

A Simple Filter

1. Use a pushpin or a compass point to poke a hole in the center of a Styrofoam hamburger tray or bowl.
2. Line the bottom of the tray with one coffee filter.
3. Use the measuring cup to pour 30 cc of fine sand on the coffee filter. Spread out the sand.
4. Use the scissors to cut one paper towel into four quadrants. Place one of the four pieces on top of the sand.
5. Cover the paper towel piece with 30 cc of charcoal such as that used in aquarium filtering systems. Spread out the charcoal.
6. Cover the charcoal with another fourth of the paper towel.
7. Use the measuring cup to pour 30 cc of gravel on top of the paper towel. Spread out the gravel.
8. Cover the gravel with another piece of paper towel.
9. Place the Styrofoam tray on top of a large, clear plastic cup. Use masking tape to keep the tray in place.
10. Pour a cup of clear water through the filter to wet it down. Watch the water as it slowly goes through the filter and drips into the glass below. Pour out the water.

Adding Impurities

11. Fill a small clear plastic cup with water. Stir in about 30 cc of dirt.
12. Slowly empty this cup of water onto the filter you have made.
    - Observe the water as it drips into the cup. What do you think made it appear clean?
    - Examine each layer of materials. Which of the materials used in the filter seemed to take much of the dirt out?
    - Make another cup of dirty water and pour it slowly through the filter. Did it work as well?

Dirty Water *(cont.)*

Adding Other Impurities

1. Fill the small clear plastic cup again with water.

2. Use the measuring cup to pour one ounce (30 cc) of cooking oil into the cup of water and stir.

3. Remove and replace the top section of paper towel on the filtering system.

4. Slowly pour the oily water over the filter and watch the water filter into the large bottom cup.

5. After the filter stops dripping water, remove the filter and examine the water in the cup.

   • Does it feel oily?

   • Can you see any oil droplets on any sections of the filter?

6. Fill the small cup with water again. Use the measuring cup to pour one ounce (30 mL) of liquid soap into the water and stir.

7. Replace the filter on the large cup.

8. Pour the soapy water over the filter and watch as it drips into the large cup. After the filter stops dripping water, remove the filter and examine the water in the cup.

   • Does it feel soapy?

   • Can you see any soap in the water or on any sections of the filter?

9. Replace the tray on the large cup. Fill the small cup again with water. Stir in some coffee or coffee grounds.

10. Pour the coffee water over the filter and observe what happens as the water drips out of the filter.

    • Can you see the coffee in the water?

    • Remove the filter and smell the water. Can you smell the coffee?

11. Replace the tray on the large cup. Fill the small cup again with water. Stir in some food coloring.

12. Pour the colored water over the filter and observe what happens as the water drips out of the filter.

    • Can you see the color in the water? Why do you think the color was not filtered out?

Dirty Water *(cont.)*

Making a Better Filter

1. Poke a hole in the center bottom of another Styrofoam hamburger tray.

2. Line the bottom of the tray with one coffee filter.

3. Spread 30 cc of fine sand on the coffee filter.

4. Use the scissors to cut each of two paper towels into four quadrants. Place one of the four pieces on top of the sand.

5. Spread 30 cc of coarse sand on the paper towel and cover this with another piece of toweling.

6. Spread 30 cc of charcoal on the paper towel and cover with another piece of toweling.

7. Spread 30 cc of gravel on top of the paper towel and cover the gravel with another piece of paper towel.

8. Spread 30 cc of sawdust on top of the paper towel and cover the sawdust with another piece of paper towel

9. Place the Styrofoam tray on top of another large, clear plastic cup. Use masking tape to keep the tray in place.

10. Pour a cup of clear water through the filter to wet it down. Pour out the water.

11. Fill a small clear plastic cup with water and stir in about 30 cc of dirt.

12. Slowly empty this cup of dirty water onto the filter you have made.

   • Observe the water as it drips into the large plastic cup. Does this water seem as clean or cleaner than the water from the first filter?

   • Examine each layer of materials. Which of the materials used in the filter seemed to take out much of the dirt?

   • Make another cup of dirty water and pour it slowly through the filter. Did it work as well?

13. Fill the small plastic cup again with water. Stir in one ounce (30 mL) of cooking oil. Remove and replace the top section of paper towel on the filtering system. Slowly pour the oily water over the filter and watch the water filter into the large bottom cup.

   • After the filter stops dripping water, remove the filter and examine the water in the cup. Does it feel oily?

   • Can you see any oil droplets on any sections of the filter?

   • Did this filter work better than the first one?

Dirty Water *(cont.)*

Stir one ounce (30 mL) of liquid soap into a cup of water and pour it on the filter. After it has filtered through, examine the water. Does it feel soapy? Can you see any soap in the water or on any sections of the filter? Test the filter with coffee water. Did the color still come through? Test the filter with food coloring and water. Did the color still come through?

Design Your Own Filter

Create your own water filtration system. Some of the ideas you might use could include the following:

- Try different papers as filters. Try facial tissue instead of a coffee filter or instead of paper towel.
- Add some components such as cotton balls or the cotton floss used in aquarium filters.
- Use some of the materials in double layers. You might use a double layer of fine sand or charcoal, for example.
- Add components such as larger gravel or aquarium gravel to the layers.
- Reorganize the layers so that sand is on top, for example, and charcoal underneath.
- Switch the layers between filtering periods to test which way works best.
- You might want to remove and replace some, several, or all of the paper layers between filtering periods.

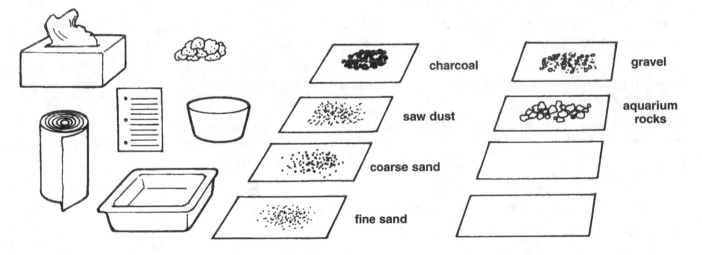

Try filtering some of these liquids as well as others you can find:

- vinegar and water
- cola and water
- baking soda and water
- tea
- potting soil and water
- a cleanser in water
- powdered laundry soap in water
- juices
- milk

Total Telegraphy

Concepts: *electricity and circuits*
Materials: batteries, flashlight bulbs, bulb holders, bell wire, rough sandpaper
Optional: battery holders

Basic Telegraph

Follow these directions to make a simple bulb telegraph using one flashlight battery, one flashlight bulb, and one piece of insulated bell wire about six inches (15 cm) long.

1. Wrap a square of rough sandpaper around one end of the wire. Squeeze, twist, and pull the sandpaper against the wire until the last inch (2.54 cm) of wire is stripped bare. Do the same on the other end of the wire.
2. Place one bare end of the wire against the bottom or negative pole of the battery.
3. Hold the base of the bulb against the top or positive pole of the battery.
4. Touch the other bare end of the wire against the metal side of the bulb. The bulb should light. Remove the wire, and the bulb goes out.

To use the international Morse code with this simple telegraph, hold the wire against the bulb for a count of one for a dot and a count of two for a dash. Use a three count between letters and a four count between words.

For example, S O S would be ● ● ● ─ ─ ─ ● ● ● with each of the dots sent by holding the wire against the bulb for a count of one and each of the dashes for a count of two.

Study the Morse code shown here. Practice sending some letters with the apparatus.

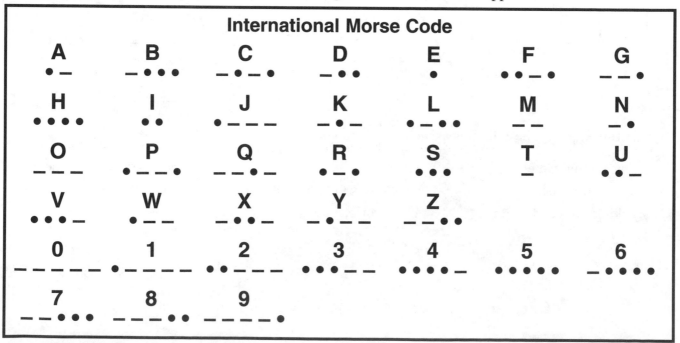

International Morse Code						
A	B	C	D	E	F	G
● ─	─ ● ● ●	─ ● ─ ●	─ ● ●	●	● ● ─ ●	─ ─ ●
H	I	J	K	L	M	N
● ● ● ●	● ●	● ─ ─ ─	─ ● ─	● ─ ● ●	─ ─	─ ●
O	P	Q	R	S	T	U
─ ─ ─	● ─ ─ ●	─ ─ ● ─	● ─ ●	● ● ●	─	● ● ─
V	W	X	Y	Z		
● ● ● ─	● ─ ─	─ ● ● ─	─ ● ─ ─	─ ─ ● ●		
0	1	2	3	4	5	6
─ ─ ─ ─ ─	● ─ ─ ─ ─	● ● ─ ─ ─	● ● ● ─ ─	● ● ● ● ─	● ● ● ● ●	─ ● ● ● ●
7	8	9				
─ ─ ● ● ●	─ ─ ─ ● ●	─ ─ ─ ─ ●				

134

Total Telegraphy *(cont.)*

Using the International Morse Code

- Use the Morse code and your simple telegraph to send your own name in code.
- Write out five three-letter words in code and practice them with the telegraph.
- Write out five of your friends' names in code and practice them on the telegraph.
- Why do you think the letters M, T, E, I, and S are easy to learn?
- Which letter do you think is the most frequently used letter in English?

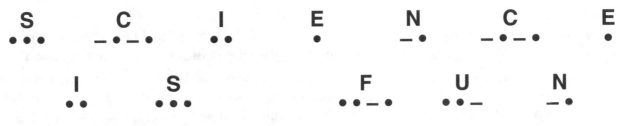

Improving the Telegraph

You can improve your telegraph by making these changes:

1. Add a bulb holder or socket to your circuit. Screw the bulb gently but firmly into the holder. Make sure the bottom of the bulb is touching the bottom metal piece of the socket.

2. Use the rough sandpaper to strip the insulation off both ends of one more wire about six inches (15 cm) long. Remember to squeeze, twist, and pull the insulation off the last inch on each end.

3. Attach one bare end of the other wire to one clip on the socket. Press down on the clip, and the wire will feed through the "eye" of the socket.

4. Attach one bare end of the other wire to the other clip in the socket in the same way.

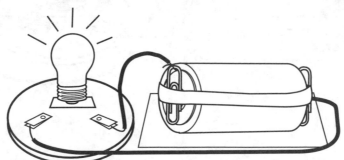

5. Press one bare end of one wire against the base or negative pole of the battery.
   - Wrap the bare end of the other wire around a large paper clip.
   - Use a rubber band to hold the paper clip against the top or positive pole of the battery. The bulb should light.
   - Use this model to send some short words.
   - Practice sending your name and the names of your friends on this set.
   - Write out three short sentences in Morse code. Send each sentence. Leave a four-count between each word.
   - Practice sending names, words, and the three sentences with a classmate.

Total Telegraphy *(cont.)*

Attaching the Battery

You can make the set easier to use by making a holder for the battery.

1. Double two medium length rubber bands to make four layers and wrap them over the poles of the battery. C or D cell batteries are easier to wrap, but AAA batteries will work.

2. Connect one wire from the socket to a large paper clip by wrapping the bare end around the middle of the clip.

3. Disconnect one wire from the socket and wrap one end of it around the middle of another large paper clip.

4. Insert one of the wire-wrapped large paper clips between the rubber band layers and the metal positive pole at the top of the battery. Be sure the paper clip is firmly held against the metal.

5. Insert the other wire-wrapped large paper clip between the rubber band layers and the metal negative pole at the bottom of the battery. Be sure the paper clip is firmly held against the metal. It is best if the wire and paper clip are both held against the pole by the rubber band.

6. Wrap the bare end of the wire extending from the battery around another large paper clip.

7. Touch the paper clip to the empty side of the socket. The bulb should light.

8. Practice your name, several words, and two sentences with this version of the telegraph.

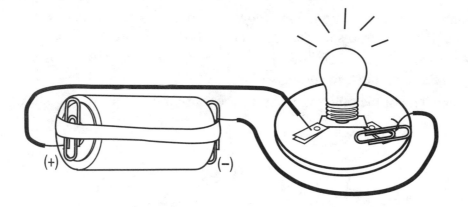

Variations

- Change the design of your telegraph so that the code is being tapped against the battery instead of the socket.
- Strip the insulation from the ends of a third wire and use it to create another working version of the telegraph.
- Make your telegraph set easier to use and more mobile by connecting it to a piece of wood or attaching it to a book with rubber bands.
- Use a plastic battery holder, if available, to connect your battery to the apparatus.
- Join a classmate or use another socket to make a telegraph with two bulbs.

Total Telegraphy *(cont.)*

Multiple Hookups

Join a classmate and hook your telegraph to your partner's so that either of you can send a message to both telegraphs. There are several ways to do this.

- Try connecting your switch (paper clip and wire) to his socket and his switch to your socket.
- Use extra wires if needed.
- Switch the socket and battery wire hookups between sets.
- Use your imagination and your understanding of the telegraph circuit to find different arrangements that will work. Draw a diagram of each one.

- Try hooking up a third telegraph set.
- Try using only two batteries and three sockets or three batteries and one or two sockets.
- Connect a fourth telegraph set.
- See how many sets you can get hooked on one desk and still send a code.
- Take turns sending a simple code with one person sending and the other decoding.

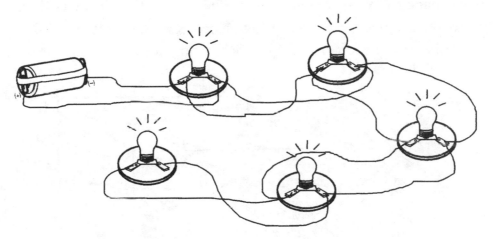

Make Your Own Code

- Design your own code either to have a secret code or to have a simpler version for sending messages. You might design a code that uses dots or dashes for whole words or phrases.
- Work out a code to use only with your partner. Practice with the code and explain how it works.

Design Your Own Telegraph

- Use the materials you've been working with and others of your choosing to create your own telegraph design with arrangements for connecting battery, bulb, and wires.
- You might consider a telegraph that clicks or buzzes, using electromagnets or other materials.
- You might design a different or better switch or use more powerful batteries.
- You might choose to connect telegraphs between two rooms or several rooms.

Vivaria for Life

Concept: *habitat needs for living things*

Materials: dirt and sod, clear habitat container, dead leaves, pillbugs, snails, earthworms, crickets, black construction paper, garlic, onion, black pepper, paper towels

Optional: various cages, plastic habitats or aquariums, other insects, lizards, frogs, toads, rodents

Getting Started

A *vivarium* is a habitat for keeping living things in as natural an environment as possible.

1. Use an aquarium or plastic habitat or a large plastic storage box for your beginning vivarium.
2. Cover the bottom of the container with at least two inches (5 cm) of potting soil or rich soil which has had plants growing in it.
3. Press clumps of grass sod or other growing plants in the dirt in one section of the container.
4. Cover the remaining soil areas with grass seed, wild bird seed, or flower seeds.
5. Cover the seeds with a fine layer of soil about one centimeter (.4") deep.
6. Use a spray bottle or small cup to thoroughly dampen the soil but do not drench it. Do not leave standing water on the soil.

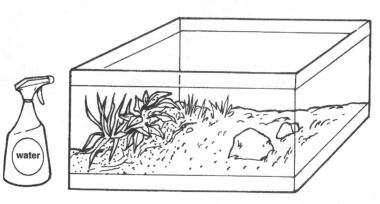

Pillbug Comforts

Pillbugs, or roly-polys, are easy animals to keep alive in your vivarium. They require little care and are fun to observe. You can find them under damp rocks or vegetation.

- Place several pillbugs in the vivarium.
- Make a small pile of dead leaves, flower petals, and grass in one section of the vivarium. Add a small rock near this dead vegetation. Keep this pile of material and rock damp every day.
- Examine the vivarium every day. Where do the pillbugs stay?
- How do they react to a small wad of wet paper towel left in the vivarium?

Vivaria for Life *(cont.)*

Snail Secrets

1. Place several snails in the vivarium and cover the top with see-through plastic wrap if you do not have a screen or lid for the container. You may also use a piece of nylon stocking. Tape the plastic or nylon stocking firmly in place. Use a pushpin or the point of a compass to punch small air holes in the plastic.

2. Leave several small piles of flower petals, leaves, clover, a lemon rind, and other similar fresh organic materials on both the grass sod and on the soil. Water the vivarium.

3. Keep the vivarium indoors in a warm part of the room. Spray the vivarium daily with water and observe results.

 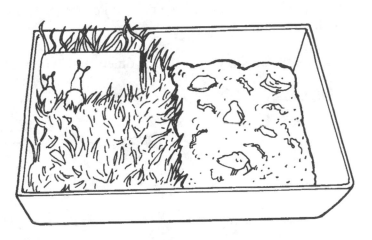

- How have the snails changed the appearance of the vivarium?
- What has been moved?
- Can you see if they have eaten any parts of the leaves, petals, grass, or other organic materials?
- Why do you think the snails sleep on the walls and the cover of the vivarium?
- Do the snails and the pillbugs seem to get along?

4. Spray the inside of the vivarium well and cover the container with a dark black paper cover for a day or two. Remove the cover and examine the vivarium.
   - Can you tell if the snails have been active?
   - Were they active when you uncovered the box?
   - Place a variety of other foods from lunches or gardens to determine if they will eat them.
   - Test whether the snails will eat or go near garlic, onion, or black pepper.

Vivaria for Life (cont.)

Earthworm Gardens

- Add several earthworms to your vivarium. Make sure the soil is damp but not drenched. Put your finger in the soil to make sure that it is wet at least two inches (5 cm) deep. Cover the top of the dirt with a variety of foods in little piles.

- Crush several different leaves and put in little piles of each leaf type. Put vegetables such as a leaf of lettuce, a few pieces of cooked corn, peas, or beans in a pile. Put a small mound of coffee grounds in another area. Try small bits of fruits such as banana, orange, lemon, or peach. Make a small pile of dead grass. Leave a pile of flower petals.

- Dampen all of the food choices.

- Clean out other materials so that you can observe how the pillbugs, snails, and worms rearrange their environment.

- Add teaspoon-sized amounts of other foods you think they will eat.

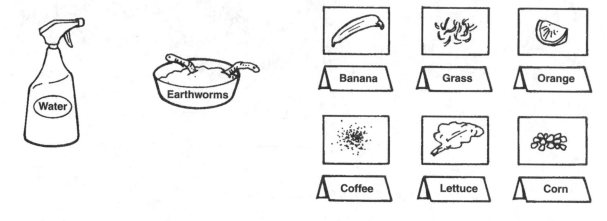

- Cover the vivarium again with a piece of black construction paper. Leave the vivarium undisturbed for two or three days. Examine the vivarium and note which foods appear to have been preferred and which appeared untouched.
- Cover the garden with the black paper again and examine it every day or two.

Insect Condominiums

Add some crickets to your vivarium. They are omnivorous and will eat several of the vegetable choices. They like oatmeal or bran cereal and chicken starter mash. Keep a small wad of damp paper towel in the vivarium. They often get their water from this or damp dead leaves.

- Make some minihouses using part of an egg carton or index cards for crickets to have the hidden areas they prefer. Crickets seem to eat almost anything, including each other. The houses help the smaller and weaker insects hide. Examine your vivarium daily.
- Which animals seem to be doing especially well?
- Which foods are disappearing?
- Can you see any sign of the earthworms?

Vivaria for Life *(cont.)*

Variations

- Observe how your vivarium changes over the course of two weeks by examining it every day.
- Add other insects and similar creatures you might find outside, such as beetles, moths, grasshoppers, and caterpillars.
- Aphids and ladybugs are also good additions. Aphids are found on flowers and tomato leaves and are food for ladybugs.
- You might add a predator. Alligator lizards and anoles are easy to obtain. If you add a predator, expect some of the insects and other creatures to be eaten.

Reminder: Clean out any foods which start to mold or stink. Keep the vivarium damp. Add sticks, pebbles, or other features to keep the vivarium interesting.

Design Your Own Vivarium

- Use the information you have acquired doing this activity to design a vivarium for other garden creatures such as frogs, toads, newts, or salamanders. Determine which animals these amphibians will eat. You might have to purchase food from a pet store for several of them. Determine which animals will get along together.
- Design and build a vivarium to meet the needs of a rodent such as a pet mouse, hamster, or rat. Determine its needs and decide how you could adapt an environment to provide food, water, exercise, and nesting materials for this rodent.

Note: Never capture or touch a wild rodent! They can be dangerous and carry deadly diseases.

Contraption Carnival

Concept: *application of science concepts*
Materials: will vary widely by project
Optional: will vary according to need

Getting Started

Design a contraption or invention for a classwide contest and presentation.

The general instructions are as follows:

1. You must define a need for the product.
2. It should not be something that people already have unless your design is different.
3. You must make a model of the product and list the materials used. Materials must be available at school or at home.
4. You must make a presentation to the class, demonstrating the use of the product.
5. You need to determine who would purchase a contraption of this nature, where it would be sold in stores, and what a reasonable price for the product might be.

Brainstorming

Think of all of the things you have said somebody ought to invent. Consider irritations or troublesome problems that you might face in school or at home. Think about your daily activities from the time you get up until you go to bed. Make a list with your partner of all of the things which come to mind, even silly or unusual suggestions.

Think of problems you might have with chores at home, vehicles you ride, personal care items you use, clothes you wear, your recreations and sports, and things you think would be a good idea to combine.

Contraption Concepts

Here is a list of suggestions to use as a springboard for creating your own contraption or unique invention.

1. an automatic toothpaste dispenser so you don't waste toothpaste
2. a combination barrette and ponytail holder
3. a combination hatrack and nose scratcher
4. an automatic babysitter for a little sister or brother
5. a doll washer
6. a dispenser for throwing birdseed at weddings
7. a self-propelled lawn sprinkler
8. a lunchbox burglar alarm
9. a training skateboard for new skateboarders
10. a silent alarm that wakes you

Contraption Carnival *(cont.)*

Contraption Concepts *(cont.)*

11. a device for reading under the sheets after lights out
12. a tennis ball thrower for practicing
13. an organizer for every school need
14. a one-stop chair for relaxation with all needs within arm's reach
15. an automatic watering system for indoor plants
16. a prediction machine for telling fortunes
17. a combination bird feeder and bird watching machine
18. an automatic feeder for pets
19. a combination shoe polisher and foot tickler
20. a combination bike helmet and drink holder
21. a baby-naming machine
22. a combination chair and nose tickler
23. a pair of glasses that can see behind you
24. a pet washing and drying machine

Choosing the Idea

- Look over your list of ideas. Highlight two or three ideas for serious consideration.
- Draw a blueprint or diagram for each of the ideas you are considering.
- Make a list of materials or equipment you would need for making each contraption.
- List alternative materials you could use for those which are unavailable.
- Eliminate dangerous or impossible materials.
- Make your final choice.
- Make a list of the supplies and equipment that each of you is going to bring from home.
- Double-check that you have covered every possible need.
- Get your teacher's final approval for your project.

Making the Model

- Assemble your materials.
- Study your diagram.
- Make any changes you realize need to be made.
- Use care and common sense in putting your project together.
- Make sure that glue and tape are firmly applied.
- Try different types of tape to make sure the most adhesive one for this project is used.
- Reinforce any connections that you can with double layers of straw, sticks, tape, glue, or string.
- Measure carefully as you go and make alterations as you progress.
- Don't get held up on one problem area.
- Keep going on the project and ask the teacher and classmates for suggestions for solving your problem.

Contraption Carnival *(cont.)*

Testing and Retesting the Model

- Once your original model is built, you need to test the model to determine problem areas. Use the techniques you learned in this class for modifying and improving models.
- Review the concepts of strengthening geometric figures, extending the length and strength of straws, making better axles for moving toys, propelling objects with balloons and momentum, reducing friction, and using air and water pressure.

Final Questions:

- Does the model work freely or get stuck at some point?
- Did you accomplish what you set out to do?
- Is every part safe? (Make sure that nothing can pinch fingers, snap accidentally, or spill messy liquids, for example.)
- Have you asked classmates to try out your contraption and suggest ideas for improvement?
- Have you tried another variation of your model—adding a capability or advantage it didn't originally have?

Making the Presentation

- Plan your presentation for the class to include the selling points of this particular contraption. Explain why people would really want or need this device and specify which people would be particularly attracted to it. For example, someone who owned a hamster might enjoy a two-level hamster house with a built-in elevator, even if it did have to be hand-operated.
- Indicate the problems you encountered in building the model and how you overcame them by substituting materials, trying a different approach, or getting advice on how to mechanically improve the operation of the model.
- Suggest where you think a product like this might be sold and how much it would cost to produce the model using the materials you used.
- Write a commercial for your product that you think would attract buyers and interest television viewers or radio listeners.

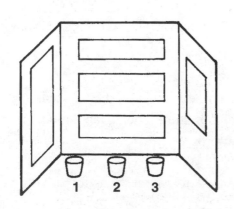